M2148 R
MORRIS, PAUL
Y0000852

D0834729

The Corinthian Correspondence

RUSSELL P. SPITTLER

Radiant BOOKS

Gospel Publishing House/Springfield, Mo. 65802

02-0892

To My Parents

Russell Paul Spittler, Sr.

Helen Virginia Spittler

Who First Taught Me To Love The Scriptures

© 1976 by the Gospel Publishing House, Springfield, Missouri 65802.
Adapted from *First and Second Corinthians* by Russell P. Spittler, © 1964 by the Gospel Publishing House. All rights reserved. Library of Congress Catalog Number: 75-43157
ISBN 0-88243-892-1. Printed in the United States of America.

A teacher's guide for individual or group study with this book is available from the Gospel Publishing House. (Order No. 32-0166).

Foreword

Few Biblical books so keenly apply to the church within modern western culture as do First and Second Corinthians. The church they address was a five-year-old charismatic congregation in a leading city the size of Long Beach.

Church and city affected each other. A Christian church still exists in the modern city of Corinth. But the city has dwindled to a Mediterranean tourist stop of 20,000 inhabitants.

The aim of these chapters is to sketch the literary content and modern relevance of the two Corinthian letters of the apostle Paul.

This series of studies began with materials prepared for the Christian Faith Series. I am grateful to the editors of the Gospel Publishing House for the opportunity of putting them in paperback form.

Special thanks to my secretary, Miss Laura Jarvis, for her usual typing efficiency.

RUSSELL P. SPITTLER
SOUTHERN CALIFORNIA COLLEGE

Contents

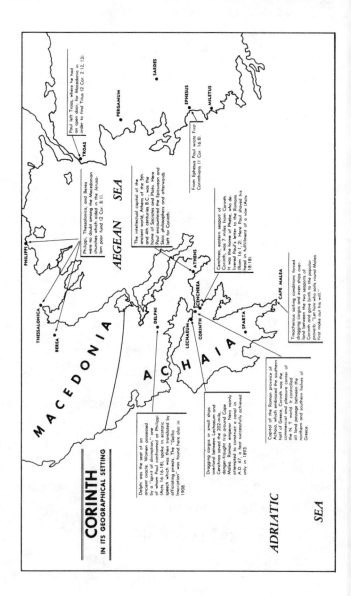

CORINTH
IN ITS GEOGRAPHICAL SETTING

ADRIATIC SEA

AEGEAN SEA

MACEDONIA

ACHAIA

Paul left Troas, where he had an open door, in order to find Titus (2 Cor. 2:12, 13).

Philippi, Thessalonica, and Berea were no doubt among the Macedonian churches which aided in the Jerusalem poor fund (2 Cor. 8:1).

The intellectual capital of the ancient world, Athens of the 5th and 4th centuries B.C., was the home of Socrates and Plato. Here Paul encountered the Epicurean and Stoic philosophers and afterwards left for Corinth.

From Ephesus Paul wrote First Corinthians (1 Cor. 16:8).

Cenchrea, eastern seaport of Corinth, was 7 miles from Corinth. It was the home of Phebe, who delivered Paul's letter to the Romans (Rom. 16:1, 2). Here Paul shaved his head in fulfillment of a vow (Acts 18:18).

Treacherous sailing conditions forced dragging cargos and even overland between the two seaports of Corinth and gave birth to the popular proverb: "Let him who sails round Malea first make out his will."

Delphi was the seat of an ancient oracle. Women possessed by a "spirit of divination," one of whom Paul confronted at Philippi (Acts 16:16-18), spoke in ecstatic speech which was then translated by officiating priests. The "Gallio Inscription" was found here also in 1908.

Dragging cargos or small ships overland between Lechaeum and Cenchrea saved the 202-mile, danger-fraught trip around Cape Malea. Roman emperor Nero in vainly attempted to construct a canal in A.D. 67, a feat successfully achieved only in 1893.

Capital of the Roman province of Achaia, which embraced the southern half of Greece, Corinth was the commercial and pleasure center of the N.T. world. It controlled all land passage between the northern and southern halves of Greece.

TROAS
PERGAMUM
SARDES
EPHESUS
MILETUS
PHILIPPI
THESSALONICA
BEREA
DELPHI
ATHENS
LECHAEUM
CORINTH
CENCHREA
SPARTA
CAPE MALEA

1

The City and the Church

Read Acts 18:1-17

Imagine a church like this one:

Members sue each other before civil courts. Others habitually attend social banquets honoring strange gods, mere idols. One brother lives in open immorality—and the church tolerates it. Others think it would be better for Christian couples to separate so they could be more "holy."

Their worship services are shocking, anything but edifying. Speakers in tongues know no restraints. People come drunk to the Lord's Supper, where they shy off into exclusive groups—each bragging about its favorite preacher. Visitors get the impression they are mad.

Some doubt the Resurrection. And many have reneged on their financial pledges.

Was there ever such a church? Yes. What's more, its founder and pastor for a year and a half was the apostle Paul!

This book examines two intimate letters sent to such a church by its pastor. First Corinthians portrays the problems of the church. Second Corinthians reveals the heart of the pastor.

How Ancient Letters Were Made

The word *epistle,* rarely used outside of Biblical circles, really means simply "letter." Paul's "epistles" are really letters—letters written for a specific purpose and in the common form for letters in that day.

Ancient letters were ordinarily written on a specially prepared material called papyrus. *Paper*—a word which comes originally from papyrus—was not used until about the 12th century. Parchment (made from specially treated animal hides) was so expensive that its use was restricted to wealthy persons or royal courts.

Papyrus was made from a water plant that grew in the Egyptian Nile River. The slender stalks were split lengthwise, cut to even lengths, and laid out side by side. A second layer was placed crosswise on top of the others. These were glued with a muddy paste and set out in the hot Egyptian sun to dry. The sizes of sheets varied, but sheets over seven or eight inches square were common, as well as larger sheets over a foot square. These were commonly pasted together to form the roll—forerunner of the modern book. Romans would have required a roll about 12 feet in length, and 1 Corinthians is just slightly shorter than Romans.

In order to bring together large collections of books, such as the Old and New Testaments, the codex was used. In the codex, sheets were stacked and laced into crude book form, permitting the collection of greater amounts of material into one unit than the roll would allow.

There is some evidence to believe that the codex displaced the roll because of the influence of the early Christians, who in the first four centuries were collecting the "books" eventually called the New Testament. Christianity has always been related to a sacred Book, and reading is a practice that has distinctively Christian overtones. "Till I come," wrote Paul to Timothy, "give attendance to reading" (1 Timothy 4:13).

CORINTH—ITS GEOGRAPHY

The city of Corinth was in a central geographical location in what is today called Greece, one of the major countries on the northern shores of the Mediterranean Sea. Today the city of Corinth thrives on the Gulf of Corinth, but the modern city is somewhat distant from the ancient site which lies in ruins.

Corinth lies on a strategic four-mile-wide neck of land (called an isthmus, from the Greek word for "neck") which divided Greece in half. All traffic moving between the northern and southern halves of Greece had to pass through Corinth—a fact that gave the city important military significance. Furthermore, on each side of the isthmus was a seaport town, thus providing inland Corinth with two seaports. To the west, on the Gulf of Corinth, was the town of Lechaeum. To the east, on the Saronic Gulf, lay the port of Cenchrea. A Christian lady named Phebe, whom Paul mentions in Romans 16:1,2 and who probably delivered his letter to the Romans, lived at Cenchrea. Acts 18:18 tells us Paul himself fulfilled a vow there.

To avoid the very dangerous sailing conditions at the tip of southern Greece, the practice was followed in Paul's day of sailing up to one of Corinth's two ports, unloading the ship's cargo and carrying it across the narrow neck of land to the opposite port, reloading there and continuing the trip, saving some two hundred miles by the land crossing. Ships that were light enough were dragged across the isthmus. The two harbors of Corinth thus brought to the city numerous travelers, merchants, and sailors, who in turn brought their religions, their wealth, and their morals (or lack of them).

CORINTH—ITS HISTORY

More than a thousand years before Christ, Corinth existed and was building the first Greek ships of war. It lay between Athens and Sparta and with them engaged in numerous wars for the control of the Greek peninsula. In 146 B.C., when the Romans were displacing Greek superiority, a general named Lucius Mummius devastated the city, and it lay in ruins for the next century. Julius Caesar, in 46 B.C., rebuilt the city, and soon it became the capital of the Roman province of Achaia which then covered half the territory of the Greek peninsula. Emperor Nero, under whom Paul and Peter were martyred, attempted unsuccessfully in A.D. 67 to cut a canal through the isthmus—a feat finally achieved only in modern times (completed 1893). In 1858 an earthquake destroyed the ruins of the ancient city.

In the world of the New Testament, few cities exceeded Corinth in commercial, political, and social significance. By coming to it Paul followed his custom of planting a Christian church in strategic urban areas from which Christianity was to spread in the years to follow.

THE LAS VEGAS OF THE ANCIENT WORLD

The harbors created the commercial importance of Corinth, which also had its own mining and pottery industries. They also symbolize the cosmopolitan character of the city—where Jews, pagans, Romans, Orientals, tradesmen, landowners, and slaves all mingled together freely.

But Corinth was also famed for its wickedness.

Atop the Acro-Corinth, a hill just south of the city and looking down over it, was a temple dedicated to the Greek goddess of love, Aphrodite. To this infamous place were attached professional prostitutes (some say 1,000) who had dedicated themselves to the goddess and amassed a fortune for the temple and thus for the city.

In fact, the Greek language developed the term *to Corinthianize,* which meant to live a life of drunken immorality. An ancient observer tells us that when Corinthians appeared on the stage in Greek plays they were always cast as drunken rakes. A "Corinthian" in ancient Greek had about the meaning that "playboy" has in modern English.

It is not a paradox to find the Corinthians interested also in athletics. The Greeks valued highly the human body, and this appears in their recreation and art as well as in their moral laxity. At Corinth were held every two years, from the sixth century before Christ, the famed "Isthmian Games"—second in popularity only to the Olympic Games held in another part of Greece. The games also included parades and amusement facilities, and the festivities constituted a major celebration similar to a state or county fair in our day.

Intellectually, Corinth did not rank with Athens, the great philosophical capital of antiquity. Rather, Corinth's major interests were, as someone has bluntly stated it, "Making money and making love."

How History Helps

Of what value are all these historical and geographical details? How do they help to understand the letters of Paul to the Corinthians? Is there anything "spiritual" about history and geography?

Here is a series of passages taken from the epistles

11

of Paul to the Corinthians. Observe how the passages receive much more meaning when the background for each, briefly summarized before each quotation, is grasped.

1. In the central part of the city of Corinth stood the ornate Temple of Apollo, some columns of which remain to this day. On the hill above Corinth stood the luxurious Temple of Aphrodite. Greek temples often contained images of the gods, whom the Greeks always pictured as humans of heroic character. How easily the Corinthians would have understood Paul when he wrote these words:

First Corinthians 3:16: "Know ye not that ye are the temple of God, and that the Spirit of God dwelleth in you?" 1 Corinthians 10:19,20: "What say I then? that the idol is any thing, or that which is offered in sacrifice to idols is any thing? But I say, that the things which the Gentiles sacrifice, they sacrifice to devils, and not to God: and I would not that ye should have fellowship with devils."

2. The Isthmian Games held near Corinth brought boxing and wrestling contests, discus and javelin throwing, footraces and broad-jumping. To people who had seen such games, Paul writes in athletic language:

First Corinthians 9:24-27: "Know ye not that they which run in a race run all, but one receiveth the prize? So run, that ye may obtain. And every man that striveth for the mastery is temperate in all things. Now they do it to obtain a corruptible crown; but we an incorruptible. I therefore so run, not as uncertainly; so fight I not as one that beateth the air: but I keep under my body, and bring it into subjection: lest that by any means, when I have preached to others, I myself should be a castaway."

3. With the cult of Aphrodite and the notorious loose morals of Corinth in mind, how significant become Paul's words to the Christians of Corinth contrasting their present with their past condition:

First Corinthians 6:9-11: "Know ye not that the unrighteous shall not inherit the kingdom of God? Be not deceived: neither fornicators, nor adulterers, nor effeminate, nor abusers of themselves with mankind, nor thieves, nor covetous, nor drunkards, nor revilers, nor extortioners, shall inherit the kingdom of God. And such were some of you: but ye are washed, but ye are sanctified, but ye are justified in the name of the Lord Jesus, and by the Spirit of our God."

How Christianity Came to Corinth

You can read the full story of the founding of the church at Corinth in Acts 18:1-17. Recall that the previous chapter describes the famous "Mars' Hill" sermon given by Paul at Athens. The results of this sermon were apparently disappointing to the apostle. We are not told that a church was founded there. Acts 17:34 names one man and one woman and cites several other men who believed. First Corinthians 2:1-5 appears to indicate that the apostle changed his method of approach upon arriving at Corinth. His philosophical sermon at Athens had not secured the desired results. To Corinth he came, as he later wrote to the church he founded there, "determined not to know any thing among you, save Jesus Christ, and him crucified" (1 Corinthians 2:2).

Arriving alone in Corinth (Silas and Timothy had stayed behind in Macedonia [Acts 17:14]; they were to join him shortly in Corinth [Acts 18:5]), Paul worked at his tentmaker's trade. He stayed with and may have been employed by Aquila and Priscilla. As his custom was, he preached first in the Jewish synagogue, convincing the Jews that the Carpenter of Galilee was indeed the longed-for Jewish Messiah.

When the Jews rejected the message, Paul moved next door to the house of a man named Justus—a move that hardly pleased the synagogue. The irate Jews hailed Paul before Gallio, who was the political leader of the province of Achaia and was appropriately situated in its capital, Corinth. Gallio threw the Jewish case out of court, at once providing the Christians with legal precedent to freely propagate their faith and demonstrating the famous equality of Roman law. (Only later, when Christian claims became more threatening to the welfare of the Roman Empire, did Roman persecution develop.)

Crispus (mentioned also in 1 Corinthians 1:14) was the lay leader of the Jewish synagogue, and his conversion ("with all his house") was a significant stage in the establishment of the Christian church at Corinth. "And many of the Corinthians hearing believed, and were baptized" (Acts 18:8).

An interesting discovery made in 1908 shows how ancient documents are dated. At Delphi, a city to the north, across the Gulf of Corinth, an inscription was found in the form of a letter from the Emperor Claudius in which he refers to his friend Gallio. By calculating the years of the emperor's reign mentioned in the inscription, scholars have determined that Gallio must have come to his proconsulship in A.D. 51 or 52. From this we know that Paul's stay in Corinth must then have been from about the spring of A.D.. 50 to the fall of A.D. 51. It was, incidentally, about this time that Paul wrote his two letters back to the church at Thessalonica upon hear-

14

ing the reports of Silas and Timothy. (Compare Acts 17:14,15; 18:5; 1 Thessalonians 1:1; 2 Thessalonians 1:1).

"YET CARNAL"

Here is an amazing paradox: Paul calls the Corinthians brethren, identifies their Lord as his, commends them for their possession of gifts and for their expectant hope for the return of the Lord. Yet he must still address them as carnal—immature believers (1 Corinthians 1:2,5,7; 3:1; 6:11; 12:2).

The character of the Corinthian congregation was dominantly pagan (what the Bible generally calls "Gentile"), though there were Jews among them. They were common people for the most part (1 Corinthians 1:26). In spite of their high calling and their gifted status, they had conspicuous moral faults.

One of the enduring lessons of a study of the Corinthian letters is the disturbing possibility of low moral standards accompanying a high interest in spiritual gifts. Paul's letters contain the solution to the problem of living an adequately Christian life in a dominantly pagan culture.

WHY THE CORINTHIAN LETTERS WERE WRITTEN

Four or five years after Paul had left Corinth, during his stay in Ephesus (which was two or three days sailing across the Aegean Sea from Corinth), reports reached Paul about some disorders among the Corinthians. These came from the circles of a Corinthian lady named Chloe, and possibly from three men who had just come to Paul from Corinth (1 Corinthians 1:11; 16:17). Paul had apparently written an earlier letter (referred to in 1 Corinthians 5:9), which has not come down to us—as also has not the epistle Paul sent to the church of the Laodiceans

(Colossians 4:16). In addition, the Corinthians had sent a letter to Paul asking about some questions (1 Corinthians 7:1).

In answer to these reports and to the Corinthian letter of inquiry, Paul wrote the first letter to the Corinthians about 25 years after the ascension of Jesus.

Not long after, when he had gone to Macedonia to met Titus who was bringing back news about the state of the Corinthian church, he wrote 2 Corinthians to express his joy over apparent improvements and at the same time to defend himself against certain charges. As no others, the two Corinthian letters "take the lid off" a New Testament church, baring to our view the problems of parish and pastor.

2

The Foolishness of Preaching

Read 1 Corinthians 1-4

Here is a summary of the sequence of thought in 1 Corinthians 1 to 4. The balance that follows the summary consists of an exposition of 1 Corinthians 1:18 to 2:16. The rest of 1 Corinthians 1 to 4 will be treated in the next chapter.

After the usual opening greeting (1:1-3) and expression of thanks (1:4-9), Paul urges abandonment of their quarrels over favorite preachers (1:10-17). He is thankful he did not baptize very many of them, so that few would pick him as their favorite (1:14-17). Apparently, this habit of preferring preachers arose from a warped conception of human wisdom —understandable in the light of the Greek appetite for philosophy. But God's wisdom, he goes on to show (1:18-25), exceeds that of men—who can only interpret the Cross as folly. God, as a matter of principle (to exclude human boasting), chooses foolish things to perplex the wise. This is illustrated first in the inferior intellectual and social status of the Corinthians themselves (1:26-31), then in Paul's own plain manner of preaching (2:1-5).

Despite the fact that the preaching of Christ crucified is "foolishness," there is a true wisdom (2:6-9) disclosed by the Holy Spirit (2:10-13) but unperceived by unspiritual persons (2:14-16).

17

Among these, surprisingly, are the Corinthians themselves (3:1-3)—as their quarrelsome divisions prove (3:4,5). They must realize that all ministers are fellow workers and that God alone causes spiritual life and growth (3:6-9). Paul laid spiritual foundations in Corinth, and others (whether individual Corinthians or their teachers) should exercise care in building up "God's building" (3:9)—which, more than a building, is a temple of God, and whoever destroys it will himself be destroyed by God (3:10-17).

Whoever therefore *really* wishes to be wise will recognize that all preachers are his; so why should he restrict himself to any one of them? (3:18-23). Rather, the Corinthians must come to see that ministers are God's stewards and that His judgment alone counts, not the opinions of their fellowmen or even their own self-estimates (4:1-5).

This all applies to Paul and Apollos (4:6), but the Corinthians are too self-satisfied to see this—a fact standing in strong contrast to the trials of the apostles (4:7-13). He writes therefore giving them fatherly advice, promising to come to them shortly but sending Timothy in the meanwhile (4:14-21).

A WARPED CONCEPTION OF WISDOM

The first disorder in the Corinthian assembly that Paul seeks to correct arose from the interest in oratory and philosophy popular at the time. The Corinthians breathed something of the spirit of neighboring Athens; so that when Apollos—"an eloquent man" (Acts 18:24)—came from Alexandria, an Egyptian city where oratory and learning flourished, an "Apollos party" formed. Others preferred Paul's less fancy style of preaching. Still others took Peter as their

18

favorite, while some (who may have been in Jerusalem some 25 years earlier and actually heard Jesus preach) formed a "Christ party."

This favoritism got beyond the bounds of personal preference and actually produced quarrels. Paul remarked (1:16,17) that he was glad he had not baptized many and thus provided no rallying point for his own "party." His mission, he declared, was not to baptize at all but to preach—and to preach without flowery eloquence.

HOLY FOOLISHNESS

The message of the Cross appears foolish to the minds of ordinary men. This is what the Bible itself says (1:18). Paul's determination was to focus his preaching on "Jesus Christ and him crucified" (2:2).

How would the ancient world react to the message that here, crucified on a cross, was One who was God suffering for all mankind? This world consisted, broadly speaking, of Jews and Greeks. While the Romans ruled both the Greeks and the Jews, their fame consisted in their statesmanship—the Greeks were the thinkers. Greek slaves were often tutors of the children of wealthy Romans.

To the Greeks, lovers of wisdom, the idea of a crucified Saviour was scandalous nonsense—certainly no striking piece of logic. To the Jews, whose Scriptures in one place read, "For he that is hanged is accursed of God" (Deuteronomy 21:23), the crucified Saviour was repulsive, even blasphemous. How could God be a man? But to both Jews and Greeks who felt God's call, the suspended Saviour was both "the power of God, and the wisdom of God" (1:24).

God's call makes the difference; it converts apparent foolishness into genuine wisdom.

The status of the Corinthians illustrates the principle that God's wisdom looks foolish in the eyes of the world. Paul has just announced two divine principles: (1) God cannot be known by sheer human effort; (2) God's ways appear foolish to unspiritual men. To illustrate these principles, Paul appeals to the Corinthians as well as himself. They themselves are not famous intellects, and he himself does not preach "with enticing words of man's wisdom."

In verses 26-28 Paul draws a precise parallel between what the Corinthians are not and what God chooses. We can see the correspondence by setting down the terms side by side:

Verse 26		*Verses* 27,28
The Corinthians are not:	God chooses:	In order to:
1. wise (intellectual)	foolish things	confound (perplex) the wise
2. mighty (powerful, influential)	weak things	confound the things which are mighty
3. noble (aristocratic, from royal families)	base (insignificant) things; things that are not	bring to nought the things that are (overthrow the things that exist)

Of course, the gospel is not limited to the lower classes. Erastus the "chamberlain" (city treasurer) was numbered among the Corinthian converts (Romans 16:23, written from Corinth). Sergius Paulus, the governor of Crete, was a convert (Acts 13:7,12) and there were numerous "chief women" (Acts 17:4, 12). But it has always remained true that "the common people heard him gladly" (Mark 12:37).

To those who believe, Christ becomes wisdom. Human intellectual effort is excluded. Not all believers have high IQ's. But receiving the grace of God is not a matter of intelligence anyway. It is from God that we receive Christ "who of God is made unto us wisdom, and righteousness, and sanctification, and redemption" (1 Corinthians 1:30).

The glorious feature of the gospel is that it is given to those possessing, not intellect, but faith—a childlike dependent trust in God. And this faith itself is a gift of God. For after all, truth is not exclusively a matter of encyclopedic facts nor even of correct theories. Truth for the Christian is not merely a statement but a Person—the Person who said, "I am the truth" (John 14:6). This one, who is himself the truth, God makes the believer's wisdom. Wise statesman or humble farmer—through faith Christ becomes their wisdom.

As Eugenia Price has said, "The ground is level at the foot of the Cross."

All this of course does not mean Christians are not to engage in disciplined thinking and persistent study. Christians, having the highest interest in the truth, should be the first to pursue it by every means congenial to Christian principle. This is the reason behind Christian schools and colleges. We are bidden to "gird up the loins" of our minds (1 Peter 1:13).

The reason God chose the foolish things to confound and perplex the wise appears in verse 29: "That no flesh should glory in his presence." *Flesh* here refers to human beings, and *glory* means "boast." If God had permitted man to attain saving knowledge of himself through the efforts of human wisdom

21

alone, we humans could brag about how we came to learn of God through our own works. But this is not God's way.

Paul's Plain Preaching

The principle of "God's foolish wisdom" is illustrated also in Paul's manner of preaching. Paul came to Corinth from Athens (some 50 miles distant) where his preaching success on Mars' Hill had not been all he could have hoped for. So far as we are told he met there neither strong opposition nor outstanding success (no church was founded at Athens). His message slanted to the Stoic and Epicurean philosophers seemed to have little effect.

So when Paul reached Corinth he was, as Phillips translates, "nervous and rather shaky." If he had spoken in philosophical terms at Athens, he determined to focus his Corinthian preaching on one theme alone: Christ crucified. Doing so, he used the "foolishness of preaching," the method labeled "folly" by men but blessed by God with effective saving power.

1 Corinthians 2:1-2 tells how Paul *did not* preach among the Corinthians, while verses 3 and 4 tell how he *did* preach. Any experienced preacher will confirm that his most effective sermons were those delivered "in weakness, and in fear, and in much trembling." And the times when he thought he had unleashed a "stemwinder" were probably among the least effective of his addresses.

The purpose of preaching is to root faith, not in man's wisdom, but in God's power. Paul preached "in demonstration of the Spirit and of power" (2:4). The Greek word here translated "demonstration" (which does not occur elsewhere in the New Testament) really means "proof." Paul did not need to resort to oratorical trickery, and as he later stated about his ministry at Corinth, "Truly the signs of an apostle were wrought among you in all patience, in signs, and wonders, and mighty deeds" (2 Corinthians 12:12).

There is a delicate line between preaching so as to attract hearers through oneself to Christ, and preaching resulting in the formation of a personal following. Even though Paul strongly reprimanded the Corinthians for picking favorites among their ministers (1:10-17), he could—without violating his own advice—say with fatherly concern: "Be ye followers of me" (1 Corinthians 4:15,16; compare 11:1).

THE SPIRIT'S WISDOM

Spiritual secrets are available to mature Christians (1 Corinthians 2:6-14). Though the gospel comes not with words of human wisdom, there is a "spiritual wisdom" for insiders—"them that are perfect." *Perfect* here means, not "flawless," but "ripe, developed." Not far from Corinth was the city of Eleusis. Here were celebrated annually the famed Eleusinian Mysteries—religious rites in which applicants were initiated into secret proceedings not fully known to this day. Those so initiated were called "the perfect," and it is doubtless to people well acquainted with the term—perhaps some initiates had become Christians— that Paul says he too offers spiritual secrets such as never entered the heart of man.

The higher wisdom is disclosed by the Holy Spirit. Who knows the innermost thoughts of man but the man himself? Likewise, it is the Holy Spirit of God who searches out the deeper thoughts of God and unfolds them to the mature (2:10,11). Only the truly mature, the truly "spiritual," can fathom these mysteries. The natural man, who knows not the revealing work of the Holy Spirit, cannot perceive these thoughts. They are just so much divine foolishness to him—just as the Cross itself is.

Surprisingly, the Corinthians themselves were still "natural" and could not share in the higher wisdom. This is the startling message of 1 Corinthians 3:1-3. "Ye are yet carnal," says Paul. They still could not delve into the true wisdom of God. Instead, they were quarreling over preacher favorites! And all this in spite of the fact that they were wonderfully endowed with spiritual gifts (1:7)!

There arises thus a provocative challenge to Pentecostal and charismatic Christians, whether in the first or in the 20th century. In spite of the presence and operation of spiritual gifts—even speaking in tongues—one may still be carnal; that is, insensitive to the revealing work of the Holy Spirit. And this revelation   of the Spirit is not way-out, mystical vision; it is simply the continuous disclosure of the things of Christ (John 16:14).

New Testament Greek—the Language of the People

True wisdom is more often the property of the common man, rather than the exclusive right of the intellectuals. This fact finds support in the very nature of the specific form of the Greek language of the New Testament. The great Swedish Biblical scholar Adolf Deissmann virtually changed the course of New Testament studies by showing the everyday character of the Greek in which most of the New Testament was written. Here are some intriguing extracts from his book, *Light from the Ancient East* (2nd ed., London, 1911): "From whatever side the New Testament may be regarded by the Greek scholar, the verdict of historical philosophy, based on the contemporary texts of the world surrounding the New Testament, will never waver. For the most part, the pages of our sacred Book are so many records of popular Greek, in its various grades; taken as a whole the New Testament is a Book of the people. Therefore we say that Luther, in taking the New Testament from the doctors and presenting it to the people, was only giving back to the people their own. . . . The New Testament was not a product of the colourless refinement of an upper class that had nothing left to hope for. . . . On the contrary, it was, humanly speaking, a product of the force that came unimpaired, and strengthened by the Divine Presence, from the lower class. This reason alone enabled it to become the Book of all mankind."

3

The Peril of Division

Review 1 Corinthians 1-4

Two seven-year-olds were sitting on a curb discussing religion. Said one to the other, "What abomination do you belong to?"

"I hear that there be divisions among you," wrote Paul to his beloved but misbehaving church at Corinth, "and I partly believe it" (1 Corinthians 11:18). He was speaking here about the haughty cliques that had formed around their celebrations of the Lord's Supper.

Earlier in the same letter (1:10-17), he told how he had heard that these cliques seemed to stem from the unwise habit of picking favorite preachers—and quarreling with those who preferred someone else!

Disunity in the local church is a problem not limited to modern times. We find this example of it even within the pages of the New Testament (which should prod the thinking of any who have too glamorous a view of "the Early Church": the saints of the Bible were as human, and sometimes as inhuman, as we are!) What is more, this was a Pentecostal church, a charismatic center in Corinth!

SOCIAL VARIETIES

From what roots came this tare of disunity at Corinth? First recall the cosmopolitan character of the city. Commercial capital that it was—with its two harbors and the overland portage—and its strategic control of north-south traffic through the isthmus, Corinth attracted a population of most varied peoples. Romans, Jews, Greeks would form staple segments of the settled population, while transient shipping interests would bring to the city Orientals from Persia, Egypt, North Africa, and many other places.

A considerable distance existed between the extremes of economic status among members of the Corinthian church. Paul said there were "not many noble," or aristocratic and therefore well-to-do, among them (1:26): but he did not say "not any." From 1 Corinthians 11:18-22 we conclude that the more wealthy were overriding the poor and making feasts of the Lord's Supper. It is generally thought that Erastus, the "chamberlain" of Romans 16:23, was the city treasurer of Corinth—not the least-paid position in any city government! Archaeologists have discovered a Latin inscription at Corinth which reads: "Erastus laid this pavement at his own expense, in appreciation of his appointment as superintendent of public works."

Still, these social, racial, and economic variations were not the only differences in the Corinthian congregation. There were also doctrinal and ethnical disunities. While Paul could commend them as a whole for keeping the teachings he had passed on to them (11:2), yet some said there is no resurrection (15:12). Others practiced the curious and obscure rite of baptism for the dead (15:29). While some misconstrued Christian liberty in such a way as to license immorality (5:1; 6:16-20), others needed Paul's advice that marriage is perfectly proper and should be sexually consummated (7:3-5).

In the light of such wide differences within the church at Corinth, it is little wonder that—in the absence of overpowering Christian love—they would start picking sides and favoring the ministers whose views most closely corresponded to their own. It is worth noticing that there was no contention among the ministers; the trouble lay in the congregation. There was as yet no resident pastor, so far as we know, though the installation of one may have been among the things Paul expected to "set in order" when he came to them (11:34).

The difference that became most troublesome at Corinth, (the one that Paul redresses in these chapters) was that of favoritism toward ministers. The Corinthian church had benefited from a wide variety of apostles and ministers—a fact not lessened by the strategic location of Corinth coupled with the wide traveling exploits of the first missionaries (2 Corinthians 1:19). Owing to the unwholesome stress on worldly wisdom, internal dissension developed when some pitted their favorite preacher against others. Thus private cliques existed in the congregation.

The Vocabulary of Variations

Three different Greek words are used to describe these Corinthian divisions. One, translated variously as "contentions" (1:11), "strife" (3:3), and "debates" (2 Corinthians 12:20), is well expressed by those words. The seriousness of these strifes becomes apparent when we discover Paul using the same word both in the catalog of vices (Romans 1:29) and in the "works of the flesh" (Galatians 5:20).

A second word, translated "heresies" in 11:19, did not yet have quite the modern meaning of "unorthodox teaching"; instead, it meant "faction" or "dissension." It was used of the sects of the Sadducees and the Pharisees (Acts 5:17; 15:5) and is also listed among the "works of the flesh" of Galatians 5:20.

The third word describing the Corinthian disunity (translated "divisions" and "schism"—1:10; 11:18; 12:25) means a tear or a rip in a cloth—such as happens when new patches are sewed onto old garments; they become "rent," that is, "torn" (Mark 2:21).

CORINTHIAN CLIQUES

Within the Corinth assembly there were unchristian cliques. Paul names four parties:

1. *The Paul party.* These were probably Gentiles, who gloried in the great principles of liberty preached by Paul as he showed how the gospel displaced the Jewish law. They were in danger, however, of misusing the liberty of Christians.

2. *The Apollos party.* Apollos was quite probably a more eloquent preacher than Paul, judging from Luke's description of him (Acts 18:24-28) and from Paul's own disavowal of oratorical excellence (1 Corinthians 2:1ff). Apollos came from Alexandria, Egypt, a famed city of learning. Both a vast library and a university are known to have existed there. The Jewish translation of the Hebrew Scriptures into Greek (which became the version used by Jesus and the Early Church) was prepared in Alexandria. Those who were impressed by the brilliant eloquence of Apollos were probably the ones who held too high a regard for sophisticated worldly wisdom.

3. *The Cephas party.* Little is known of this party. Cephas is the Aramaic (the dialect of Hebrew used as the spoken language of the Jews of this time) term for Peter. Acts tells nothing of Peter preaching in Corinth, but his popularity among Jewish

29

Christians could mean that the Jews of Corinth attached themselves to this party. Apparently the Paul party and the Apollos party were the dominant ones. Only they are mentioned when Paul brings up the matter again (3:5,6; 4:6), except that all four parties are alluded to in 3:21-23 where Paul stresses that all ministers are for all believers.

4. *The Christ party.* Still less is known of this party. We know of no visit of Christ to Corinth. This may well have been the vainest party of all. Others attached themselves to *human* preachers, but *they* were for Christ.

First Century Backgrounds

In the world of the New Testament, during the first century, certain tendencies appeared that help explain the situation at Corinth. Sects were common. Even the Jews had their "scribes, Pharisees, and Sadducees." Many of the Greeks who were concerned with serious thinking sided with such groups as the Stoics, the Epicureans, and the Cynics. The Cynics and the Stoics went about holding street meetings and preaching their own brand of morality. These groups and schools founded by Plato and Aristotle existed at Athens.

But among the people in the latter half of the first century there arose a revival of what is called the "New Sophistic"—a movement reviving an earlier (fifth, fourth centuries B.C.) interest in argument with little reference to truth. Of this movement, one classical scholar writes: "Its adherents believed that the orator, and not the philosopher, represented the highest type of man, and that the content of the oration did not matter so much as did the rhetorical skill shown by the speaker." How this affected the Corinthian church becomes clear when we learn that oratorical contests were held in conjunction with the Isthmian Games at Corinth.

Furthermore, there were all sorts of fake prophets about. One named Alexander headquartered in Aquila's homeland (Pontus). Through sheer deception he claimed to have miraculously changed an egg into a grown serpent. Gullible seekers freely lined his pockets in exchange for allegedly divine advice. Acts 8:9ff; 16:16ff; 19:13ff all show how the apostles encountered such magicians.

Thus the Corinthian church flourished in a world where attachment to individual miracle-workers was common and affiliation with "schools of thought" was routine. But Paul had to show that the Corinthian believers were members, not of a school, but of the body of Christ. Their internal dissensions mirrored only too well the world about them.

THE CAUSE OF DIVISION

What caused such unchristian divisions among Christians—Pentecostal Christians at that? A major factor was the prevalent distorted notion about worldly wisdom. But this was a result of a still deeper cause.

The Corinthians, at least some of them, were spiritually immature. This may be embarrassing for us to admit. But that is what the New Testament says; and if we accept it elsewhere, we must accept it here. Even though the Holy Spirit lived within them (". . . the Holy Ghost which is in you," 6:19), they could not call from Paul the higher secrets of the Spirit available to the mature. Proof of it was their strifes— elsewhere labeled the "works of the flesh."

They had the Holy Spirit, but the Holy Spirit did not have them. This is a persistent threat for Pentecostals—then and now. Being filled with the Spirit,

31

a Biblical phrase equal to spiritual maturity, is a present-tense, continuous matter. While speaking with tongues provides the *initial* evidence of receiving the Spirit, the Corinthian example shows us the startling fact that it is not necessarily evidence of the *continuing* work of the Spirit. Paul had to direct their interest away from speaking with tongues to love— the true fruit of the Spirit which lasts forever and shows true spiritual maturity.

A misconception of human wisdom sprang from such spiritual immaturity. They were living below their spiritual privileges. Whenever that happens, it is an easy step to an outlook formed by human values.

Self-satisfied boasting naturally issues from worldly wisdom. "Knowledge puffeth up" (8:1). The striking frequency of references to boasting in these chapters is instructive. See 1 Corinthians 1:29; 3:18,21; 4:6-10, 18; 5:2,6; 8:1; 13:4. No wonder the apostle, forced to recite his qualifications as an apostle by those who challenged his authority, appears embarrassed! 2 Corinthians 10:8,13,15,16,17).

The Sure Cure

The cure to internal congregational disunity lies embedded in these chapters of 1 Corinthians. The chief points may be summarized in this way:

1. *Christ alone is the Head of the Church* (1:13-17). Paul was not crucified for them. Who baptized a believer was unimportant. Jesus (John 4:1ff) and probably Peter (Acts 10:48) did not, and Paul did not generally baptize. The Corinthians needed to learn that they were "all baptized into one body" (12:13).

2. *God alone originates and perpetuates spiritual life* (3:5-9). The ministers are God's fellow workers,

32

His agents. The Church is "God's farm"—the real meaning of 3:9, "husbandry." Ministers can plant or water, but only God can give the increase (cause the growth). Moral: why then attach oneself to this or that minister?

3. *The coming judgment before Christ should prompt painstaking care in securing spiritual growth* (3:10-17; *compare 2 Corinthians 5:10*). In this passage there lies a warning for those at Corinth who were undoing the foundations laid by the apostle. The Church is God's temple (3:17), His building (3:9), and those threatening to destroy it by their divisive tactics are themselves in danger of destruction. They may in the end be saved, but only by fire—as if snatched from a burning house with nothing saved but themselves. Let all therefore do quality work in God's building.

4. *All ministers are given to the Church, so why limit yourself to any one of them?* This is the essence of Paul's words in 3:21-23. They were saying: "I am of Paul, or Cephas, or Apollos." He now tells them these all are for them, and they are Christ's, then God's. Not "I am of Apollos"; but "Paul, Peter, Apollos, Christ, God—are for me!"

5. *God's approval outweighs the valuations of both one's fellowmen and one's own heart* (4:1-7). Since all the ministers are for all the Corinthians, they should recognize that the ministers are God's stewards—"trustees of the secrets of God," as Phillips so aptly translates. Since they, as stewards, are responsible to God, then His judgment alone counts. So Paul says it matters little with him if others judge him (4:3). He has a clear conscience, yet he knows this is not the basis of his approval to God (4:4).

6. *Diversity is not division* (12:4-11). Diversity is divine: division is devilish. Diversity within unity

33

is God's will for the body of believers—each recognizing his individual contribution; each contributing to the underlying unity. This principle is beautifully illustrated in the distribution of spiritual gifts and in the unified diversity of the triune Godhead— each member of which is cited in 12:4-6. The Corinthian error lay in overstretching diversity into division.

4

Your Body—God's Temple

Read 1 Corinthians 5-7

Seven columns of the temple of Apollo stand today amid the ruins of Corinth. But there is another temple about which Paul wrote—the human body as the residence of God's Spirit.

The work of God in Christ for man extends beyond the redemption of his soul to the salvation of his body. Some religions, both ancient and modern, disregard the body and attempt to repress it, but not so Christianity. "The body is . . . for the Lord; and the Lord for the body" (1 Corinthians 6:13).

Some Christians, by their emphasis on the power of God available to secure physical healing, know of God's interest in the body. Whenever a supernatural healing occurs, God's concern for the body is illustrated. But not only the cure of physical ills falls within the concern of the whole gospel. The daily use of healthy bodies—and particularly their use within the partnership of marriage (or in its immoral counterfeits!)—are also the subject of Biblical controls.

We have already seen the notorious immorality of the city of Corinth, typified by the infamous temple of Aphrodite overlooking the city. As a result of questions put to the apostle in their letter to him (1 Corinthians 7:1), the Corinthians received the counsels found in what easily warrants the title of "the marriage chapter of the Bible" (1 Corinthians 7). It is startling to find that they did not include in their questions the case of gross immorality which Paul brought up on the basis of a reliable report he had heard (1 Corinthians 5:1) and with which he dealt sternly.

THOUGHT SEQUENCE IN 1 CORINTHIANS 5 TO 16

Before examining the heart of this chapter, it will be useful to trace the sequence of thought in the balance of 1 Corinthians. Chapter 2 does this for 1 Corinthians 1 to 4.

Chapters 5 and 6 form a unit in which Paul addresses himself to two moral problems at Corinth. Chapter 5 deals with an instance of fornication involving a son and his father's wife (5:1,2). Paul recommends excommunication (5:3-5) and reprimands the Corinthians for their boasting (5:6-8). Then he explains that it is up to God to judge outsiders (5:9-13). Speaking of judging suggests the second problem, treated in chapter 6. The Corinthians were suing one another before heathen courts, whereas they themselves would judge both the world and angels (6:1-6). They really ought to turn the other cheek (6:7,8). Why should they permit themselves to be judged by the unjust—immoral persons of every sort, as they themselves used to be (6:9-11)? While Christians have perfect freedom in all things, this does not license immorality—since the very bodies of believers are divine temples indwelled by the Spirit of God (6:12-20).

Chapter 7 opens the second half of 1 Corinthians, the part in which Paul answers questions posed by the Corinthians in their letter to him. The questions included, if we may judge from the letter with which Paul responds, questions about marriage (chapter 7), about foods taken from animals that were slain as sacrifices for idols (8:1 to 11:1), about the conduct of public worship (11:2 to 14:40), and about the resurrection (chapter 15). The final chapter contains personal matters regarding the collection for the poor saints at Jerusalem (16:1-4), Paul's travel plans and news about Timothy and Apollos (16:5-12), a two-verse summary of the whole letter (16:13,14), personal greetings and instructions (16:15-20), and a final signature (16:21-24).

BODIES ARE TEMPLES

Local churches are temples of God. Twice in 1 Corinthians Paul speaks of Christians as the temple of God (3:16,17; 6:19). The first time he refers to the entire Corinthian church, warning that whoever builds unwisely on the foundation he has laid among them, or whoever dishonors them by divisive teaching or practice, is himself in danger of being destroyed by God. More than "God's building" (3:9), they are a special kind of building—"the temple of God" (3:16). Thus, already Paul is suggesting that the community of believers is indwelled by the holy God.

Individual believers—their very bodies—are temples of the Holy Spirit. Paul cites this startling fact as one argument against using the body for fornication (6:19; compare 6:12-20). If their bodies are the temples of the Holy Spirit, by what logic may the temple of the Holy Spirit be joined with the body of a prostitute? What a lofty estimate of the human body these words provide! And what great care then the body deserves as the residence of God by His Spirit!

37

This passage provides incidentally a guideline to a helpful principle in interpreting the Bible. Both 6:20 and 7:34 speak of the human body and spirit. Some interpreters, who usually point to 1 Thessalonians 5:23, insist that Paul taught man has three parts to his nature. But in Corinthians he speaks only of two. It is neither necessary nor profitable to make Paul conform to some specific view of the psychological structure of human nature. He is not using the terms technically, nor is he discussing directly the structure of human nature. In this regard, a look at Mark 12:30 is instructive.

We should also guard against too rigid an understanding of what is meant by the term *body* used throughout this chapter. Primarily of course, the physical, visible part of man is meant. Yet this part is never seen apart from the other part of man (or parts, if you like)—except, of course, in a corpse, which is no longer a person! Man in all his parts exists as a unit, and the point of this chapter is precisely that there is no part of this unity that is untouched both by the blessings and by the demands of the gospel.

RESURRECTION—THE FUTURE OF THE BODY

So important is the body that it will be resurrected. The exposition of this truth receives its fullest treatment in this very letter, 1 Corinthians 15. The ancient Greeks, centuries before Christ, believed that the soul would endure forever while the body would dissolve into oblivion. The Jews came to believe, increasingly throughout the Old Testament period, that the physical bodies they knew on earth would be resurrected and reunited with the soul. But it was the clearer revelation of Christianity that disclosed that the resurrection body would be a spiritual body, a body in a new order not at all subjected to the laws of current physical bodies—as the resurrection body of the Lord illustrated (Luke 24:31,36-43).

But the message of 1 Corinthians 15 is already anticipated at 6:14, where Paul argues that it is hardly fitting to use for fornication the bodies which God will resurrect.

Christians should therefore treat their bodies as instruments of divine service. The Corinthians, who were enriched with all spiritual gifts (1:7) and knew (or thought they knew!) all about the things of the Spirit, needed yet one lesson: "Therefore glorify God in your body" (6:20). This exhortation came from the same apostle who elsewhere (Romans 12:1) spoke of a "living sacrifice." Sacrificial worship involves the death of a victim; but Christians have the privilege of being alive and being a sacrifice at the same time! (See also Romans 6:12,13.)

CHRISTIAN MARRIAGE

The principle is that the urge for physical union between sexes finds its proper satisfaction within marriage. It is important to realize that this urge, as well as marriage itself, stems from the direct creation of God. God created people "male and female" (Genesis 1:27). Marriage, with the social and physical unions it involves, existed as a divine institution before the Fall, before sin entered the world. These facts cancel any thought that there is something evil within marriage itself—a view that had crept into even the Corinthian congregation.

Once sin entered, all sorts of corruptions came along—separation and divorce, immorality, warped ways of using the body. And Corinth was the immoral showplace of the ancient world. Finding problems with immorality at the new Corinthian assembly, we should hardly expect it otherwise! Our shocked surprise at the Corinthian situation betrays a lack of knowledge of the wide practice of fornication and the lightness with which it was considered in the ancient world. Paul's corrective was his doctrine of the believer's body as the temple of the Holy Spirit.

CORINTHIAN EXCESSES

There appear to have been two opposing tendencies in the Corinthian assembly, an easy conclusion in the light of their party divisions. Some pushed Paul's doctrine of freedom beyond its intended limits. They made it into a catchword—"All things are lawful unto me" (6:12; 10:23)—then tried to legitimize immorality. Since foods were for the stomach and the stomach for foods, they argued, then the body—with its urge for fornication—must be for fornication and fornication for the body (6:13). But Paul presses home the truth that the body is not for fornication but for the Lord.

The other group at Corinth took the opposite extreme. From the advice Paul gives, we may reasonably conclude that they thought physical union within marriage should be withheld (7:5), that any believer married to an unbeliever should immediately separate from him (7:12,13), or that a girl who married commits sin (7:28).

The practical counsels Paul gives in this chapter show that neither unbridled immorality nor unconsummated marriage constitutes proper Christian use of the body.

We could wish that we had from the apostle's

hand a thorough treatise on marriage and all the problems involved in it. Present-day pastors would love to have such a writing! But 1 Corinthians, as indeed the literature of the New Testament as a whole, is written for a specific purpose and to a specific group. This fact shows the down-to-earth character of the New Testament letters. In a case like 1 Corinthians, written in part as a response to a letter no longer available to us, it is (as one writer has suggested) like listening in to one side of a telephone conversation.

BELIEVERS' MARRIAGE

Whoever marries commits no sin (7:28,36), and marriage is a good corrective to rampant immorality (7:2). Within marriage each partner should share his body in physical union (7:3), but temporary abstinence is permissible for purposes of spiritual retreat if done with mutual consent and properly resumed afterwards (7:4,5). Both Paul and the Lord forbid divorce (7:10,11) among Christians.

Throughout this chapter, the reader gets the impression that Paul only reluctantly permits marriage. But we must remember that he was constantly under the assumption that "the time is short" (7:29), and he showed a natural preference that others would follow his own example. Paul was exceedingly fair-minded; he had his own preference, yet he could say, "But every man hath his proper gift of God, one after this manner, and another after that" (7:7).

Married persons naturally will be concerned for each other—in everyday matters like shopping and spending time with each other for example. Those who marry, Paul says, "shall have trouble in the flesh" (7:28). Phillips' translation puts it clearly: "Yet I do believe that those who take this step are bound

41

to find the married state an extra burden in these critical days, and I should like you to be as unencumbered as possible" (7:28; ponder Luke 14:20).

MIXED MARRIAGES

Should a Christian married to an unbeliever separate from him (or her)? "No," says the apostle. Not as long as they are willing to live together (7:12,13). Besides, the children of such a union are brought under the influences of the gospel—they are "holy" (7:14); that is, they are influenced toward God and holiness. Furthermore, the unconverted partner himself may in time be converted (7:16).

From verse 15 some interpreters conclude that remarriage is permissible where the unbelieving partner voluntarily separates from the believing partner. This is known by scholars as "the Pauline privilege." But the passage is not entirely clear as to just what is meant by "under bondage." Furthermore, additional marriages on the part of either partner would seriously complicate the situation should the unconverted partner become a Christian.

STAYING SINGLE

Immense good has been done the Christian Church through its history by persons dedicated to remaining unmarried for more extended performance of the work of the ministry. Single women have become heroines in the work of modern missions (Lillian Trasher, for example). Jesus observed that there is a place in the Kingdom for the unmarried (Matthew 19:12).

Paul's own preference, in the light of the critical times at hand and in the light of his own example, was that unmarried or widowed Corinthians remain unmarried (7:8,11,40). Widows could remarry if they chose, but only "in the Lord"—an excellent guideline for any marriage (7:39). (See also 1 Timothy 5:3-16.)

Was Paul himself married? From 7:8 it appears that he was not. On the other hand, Jewish rabbis felt it a duty to be married. As a member of the Sanhedrin, he would probably have constituted no exception to the rule that their members be married. All these requirements would be satisfied if we could assume Paul was married but became a widower before his conversion. But there is no way either to prove, or to disprove, this assumption.

The message of 7:17-24 states an important principle: Christians should pursue the gift (7:7, same word as used for gifts of the Spirit) they have from God and not try to alter it. Let them remain in the states in which they come to faith, making no strenuous and unnatural exertions to be what they are not suited to be. This does not forbid, but encourages, marriage of youth. For as they follow their calling they will naturally marry, except the few gifted who choose to remain single. The essence of the passage is that there are things of higher concern than seeking marriage or the dissolution of marriage.

5

The Limits of Liberty

Read 1 Corinthians 8:1 to 11:1

Formal dinners of state present a considerable problem to the national government at Washington, D.C. Attending such international banquets are many statesmen from widely varied cultures around the world. Jewish statemen eat pork on no day. Moslems from the Near East, Hindus and Sikhs from India, Buddhists from Burma and Japan—all have specific dietary laws and restrictions.

The problem is so great that a special office has been set up which carefully records the dietary preferences of each country's representatives. It is difficult, if not often impossible, to find a single menu suitable to all. This office then assures meals tailored to individual demands, so that no international offense is committed.

If our national government does this for its political neighbors, should Christians do less for their brothers in Christ? There are limits to Christian liberty.

THE SEQUENCE OF THOUGHT:
1 CORINTHIANS 8:1 TO 11:1

As a preparation for what follows, let us catch the drift of the apostle's thought in 1 Corinthians 8:1 to 11:1. (Note that 11:1 actually concludes 10:

33. This illustrates the first rule of Bible study: one must disregard chapter and verse divisions. These were not added until at least a thousand years after the Bible was written.)

It is true, says the apostle (8:1-6), that there is only one true God and "an idol is nothing in the world." But love excels knowledge. For there are some less mature believers who have not attained such knowledge, and to bowl them over with an unloving act of your knowledge would be to sin against Christ. So if a weaker brother might be offended in the process, better let the act go undone.

Take a personal example of how Paul used his apostolic rights (chapter 9). Though he had every right to demand financial support from those to whom he preached (9:1-12), he relinquished this right in order to go the second mile in making the gospel without charge (9:12-18). His operating principle was that he would become all things to all men, so that he might win some to God (9:19-23). Hence, he accepted no pay from the Corinthians who were plagued with money-grabbing preachers. Like an athlete, he disciplined himself through denial (9:24-27). Should not the Corinthians likewise forfeit their "rights" for the sake of others?

Take another example—this time from the fathers who, though they enjoyed high spiritual privileges under Moses (10:1-4), so insisted on their "rights" that they fell dead under God's judgment in the wilderness (10:5). Their example should be a warning to us (10:7-12), but we can always count on God's providing a way through every test (10:13).

Furthermore, the cup and the bread of the Lord's Supper link us to the body of Christ. How then can a Christian eat and drink at an idol feast? Indeed, demonic powers lurk behind the harmless images of the idols. And we must flee idolatry (10:14-22).

Summing up (10:23 to 11:1), since the whole earth is the Lord's it really does not matter what you eat. But if a weaker brother who does not yet know this would be offended by your eating, do not eat. Otherwise, buy meat at the market without asking questions and even go to an unconverted friend's house for dinner. Whatever you do, do it for God's glory and men's profit. You can follow Paul's example in this.

IDOL FEASTS AT CORINTH

At least three issues bothered the Corinthians:

1. *Should a believer eat meat which may have been slaughtered in connection with a sacrifice to an idol?* (1 Corinthians 8:7-13; 10:25,26). In the sacrifice of animals among both Jews and Gentiles, often the whole animal was not burned on the altar. A token part was, but a major portion went to the officiating priest. (For this practice in Israel, see Exodus 32:5,6; Leviticus 6:18,29; 7:6,15, and compare 1 Corinthians 10:18.) The balance of the meat might be taken home by the one who offered the sacrifice, or it might be sold to meat markets. Those who bought meat in the public markets would therefore never really know whether or not the meat originated as an idol sacrifice. Furthermore, the decisions of the first apostolic council at Jerusalem included a ban on "meats offered to idols" (Acts 15:29). Given some six or seven years earlier and circulated among the churches of Palestine and Asia Minor (Acts 15:23; 16:4), the Corinthians may have been wondering how this applied to their particular case.

2. *May a Christian accept a dinner invitation to a home where such idol-meats might be served?* (1 Corinthians 10:27-30). Paul's response to the problem of idol-meats at Corinth made several facts

clear. First, no food has any special virtue—or vice; the whole earth is the Lord's (1 Corinthians 8:8; 10:26,30; compare 1 Timothy 4:3-5). Sacrificing meat to an idol—which is no real god anyway—cannot contaminate it. It is not the meat, but where and for what purpose the meat is served that counts, and whether or not your eating will offend some weaker conscience. So—unless the origin of the meat is specifically pointed out by a weaker brother—"If any of them that believe not bid you to a feast, and ye be disposed to go; whatsoever is set before you, eat, asking no question for conscience' sake" (1 Corinthians 10:27).

3. *Can a Christian participate in the common meal of a pagan social club?* (1 Corinthians 8:10; 10:14-22). But sitting in "the idol's temple" is another matter: this draws a prohibition from the apostle. At Corinth and elsewhere in the first-century world there were many social clubs or societies. Some of these were religious, comparable to church sewing circles or to the Knights of Columbus in our day. Others, probably the majority, were primarily social in nature, having some common interest such as similar businesses (trade unions!), common home-lands ("Polish Clubs" or "Italian Clubs" in major cities today), common political goals (Young Republican Club).

The thing that bound these clubs together was the common meal they shared. More than likely some patron deity was selected from the many of the pagan world and the meal was dedicated to him —even though the purpose of the organization was not specifically to honor the god. The Roman government did not like such clubs, because Roman leaders had discovered that the loyalties of club members, secured through the ceremonious common meal, often became greater than their loyalties as citizens of the Roman Empire. This of course posed a political threat.

The Lord's Supper began as just such a common meal, which is one reason the early Christians were viewed with disfavor (notice in the setting of Mark 14:12-26 that this was an actual meal). One of the disorders at Corinth Paul had to correct (11:17-34) was that the Corinthians had permitted this sacred common meal to become a selfish, disorderly brawl. As time passed, the Lord's Supper came to be observed with the two elements of bread and wine only, apart from any meal.

Now Paul advises that to share in the Lord's Supper binds believers to Christ (1 Corinthians 10:16, 17). Therefore eating at "the table of devils" is both illogical and spiritually perilous. For in such an environment as an idol temple, demonic spirits flourish (10:20,21). And while idols are nothing in themselves, there are real devilish powers that flourish where idols are.

In summary then, Paul's advice in these three specific situations was the following: (1) Buy meat at the market without asking questions. (2) Go to an unsaved friend's house for dinner if you are inclined to, and eat what is offered unless someone raises a question of conscience. (3) Stay away from banquets in idol temples.

A GOOD EXAMPLE: PAUL'S OWN PRACTICE

Apostles had a right to financial support (1 Corinthians 9:1,2,5). But at Corinth Paul supported himself during his year-and-a-half stay through his tentmaking trade (Acts 18:3; 2 Corinthians 12:13,17, 18). He did not do this everywhere, as we may learn from Philippians 4:16,17.

Paul supported himself in order to make the gospel free of charge. It is reasonable to assume that the Corinthians were accustomed to a luxuriating clergy—perhaps some of those Christian preachers who preached for money's sake (1 Timothy 6:5; Titus 1:11; compare Philippians 1:18; 1 Timothy 3:3,8; Titus 1:7) or even the pagan priests who often made a going business of selling the pelts of the sacrificial animals. To avoid any such reproach against the gospel Paul forfeited this right to financial support (9:18). For he always became all things to all men, fitting into their habits and customs and needs, always with the one goal—to win them to God.

A Bad Example: The Fathers of Israel

The leaders of Israel enjoyed great spiritual privileges (1 Corinthians 10:1-4). They witnessed God's miraculous deliverance of the children of Israel from Egypt. They had a foretaste of the two Christian ordinances, having been "baptized" in the Red Sea and having shared in the "spiritual drink" which flowed from the divided Rock.

But these high privileges did not keep them from sin (1 Corinthians 10:5,7-10). The sins itemized in 10:7-10 are anything but what one would expect from those so privileged.

Their example issues a clear warning (10:6,12). Each of the sins mentioned by Paul could also be traced within the Corinthian congregation. Their example shows the danger of thinking that the possession of spiritual privileges is in itself unassailable spiritual security.

The whole point Paul is getting at here is this: the Corinthians, gifted in so many ways (1:5) and puffed up with their "knowledge" about the unreality of idols, had better take heed lest they fall. "To whom much is given much is required." But love "is not puffed up" (13:4—the great "Love Chapter" is already anticipated here). The real question at issue is, "through thy knowledge shall the weak brother perish, for whom Christ died?" (8:11).

1. *Whatever we do must be done to the glory of God and to the profit of men* (1 Corinthians 10:31-33). We are not to please ourselves, but to forfeit our own rights voluntarily for the sake of others. This does not mean snuffing out our own identity, nor does it involve letting others walk over us. Paul stiffly opposed his enemies yet lovingly cared for his churches. The unifying principle was the dual one —God's glory and men's upbuilding.

2. *Our acceptance with God does not depend on what we eat or do not eat* (8:8; 10:25,26). We are accepted by God through the work of Christ. Our acceptance is a matter of Christ's death, not of our diet. The whole of God's creation, as one may prefer, is fit for food. There is no food unclean in itself (Romans 14:14—the whole chapter should be read in connection with this chapter). If any brother does not eat one food, he should not seek to impose this restriction on another.

3. *We all bear, however, a responsibility to weaker brethren* (8:10-13; 10:28). We are never to fracture their faith. (See especially Romans 14:13-23.) We are our brother's keeper. "If meat make my brother to offend, I will eat no flesh while the world standeth" (1 Corinthians 8:13).

4. *Not superior knowledge, but Christian love, is the basic guide to Christian action* (8:1-3; 13:2,4). Knowledge leads to conceit, it "puffs up." But love edifies, or helps. There is nothing wrong either in

having or in acquiring knowledge. In fact, the instruction of the church is a major thrust of its work ("go ye therefore, and *teach* . . ." Matthew 28:19). But, "Though I . . . understand all mysteries, and all knowledge . . . and have not charity, I am nothing" (1 Corinthians 13:2).

5. *"What is safe for one man may be quite unsafe for another"* (8:13; 10:29). This is the way William Barclay expresses a definite spiritual law. We all vary, and God's calling may require special sacrifices of some—sacrifices that are not intended for all (staying single, for example, as we see in 1 Corinthians 7). But each man stands or falls to his own master, and we should not judge another's liberty. But we should thoroughly establish our spiritual laws by working them out with the Lord— what He requires or permits of each of us individually.

6. *"Spiritual experience does not guarantee infallibility."* This is Phillips' heading to 1 Corinthians 10:1-12. And it is a spiritual law worth remembering constantly by all Christians—particularly those who value the charismatic experience.

6

Custom-Breaking

Read 1 Corinthians 11

ANOTHER LIMIT TO LIBERTY

In America gentlemen allow ladies to go first. But in Japan, ladies allow gentlemen to precede. The difference is *custom*.

Taking as their slogan the sentence "All things are lawful to me" (1 Corinthians 6:12; 10:23), the Christ party at Corinth tried to stretch freedom into license for both immorality (6:12-20) and attendance at banquets in idol temples (8:10; 10:21). Now, in 1 Corinthians 11, we find the same spirit seeking to do away with the woman's veil and to convert the Lord's Supper into a cluster of divisive cliques.

In Paul's reply we discover another limitation on liberty—the customs of the churches. They had no right to break established religious custom—practices that stemmed ultimately from Paul's personal encounter with Christ.

THE SEQUENCE OF THOUGHT: 1 CORINTHIANS 11:2-34

The entire section from 1 Corinthians 11:2 through chapter 14 deals as a whole with disorders in worship. There were three such disorders: (1) the tendency to discard the veil (1 Corinthians 11: 2-16); (2) the cliquishness marring the Lord's Supper (11:17-34); and (3) the misuse of spiritual gifts (chapters 12 to 14).

Chapter 11 (excluding verse 1, which goes with the preceding section) forms a self-contained unit. Verses 2, 17, and the last part of 34 furnish clues to the structure of the chapter. Paul first commends the Corinthians for keeping the rules he had given them (11:2)—a very tactful way to bring up a situation in which they had fallen short! Then he speaks about the reasons women should retain their veils (11:3-16). In 11:17 he says he cannot praise them (as he could in verse 2) about the way in which they are observing the Lord's Supper—their coming together is harmful, not helpful. Then he proceeds to describe their error (11:18-22), reminding them of the right way to observe the Lord's Supper (11:23-26). Then Paul brings out the principle of judgment (11:27-32). He advises them in conclusion to satisfy hunger at home, preferring one another at church (11:33,34).

How interesting it would be to know just what Paul had in mind when he closed this section of his letter with the words, "And the rest will I set in order when I come"! (1 Corinthians 11:34).

First Corinthians 11 therefore treats the first two disorders that spoiled the worship of the Corinthian assembly.

WOMEN'S LIB AT CORINTH

Certain women in the church at Corinth wished to do away with wearing veils. As suggested earlier, these women were probably associated with the group at Corinth that was overstepping the bounds of liberty. By doing away with the veil the women were striving for a degree of equality with men virtually unknown in the ancient world. Among the Jews both men and women prayed with covered heads out of reverence to God. In 2 Corinthians 3:13

53

reference is made to Moses' use of the veil. The Greeks, however, carried out their sacrifices to their many gods without any head coverings; they did not have the high sense of reverence characteristic of the Jews.

Though the exact form of the veil under discussion here is not clear to us (though it was of course so clear to the Corinthians as to require no elaboration), several facts are clear. First, women of the Bible lands commonly wore veils dropping to the toes from the eyes. In many areas, this is still done. The veil was a sign of modesty. It was not worn by prostitutes such as the hundreds associated with the temple of Aphrodite at Corinth.

Women were separated from men in the Jewish synagogue to which Paul customarily first went on his preaching missions. This practice doubtless influenced the earliest Christian churches in structure and organization. But in the Christian community, in response to Paul's message that "there is neither male nor female: for ye are all one in Christ Jesus" (Galatians 3:28), women had even come to lead in prayer and to preach (1 Corinthians 11:5). But this freedom plunged them into the peril of disregarding a natural order found even within the Trinity (1 Corinthians 11:3). As we learn from 1 Corinthians 14:34,35, they were noisily quizzing their husbands—an obvious disorder if the Corinthian assembly separated the men and the women into opposite sides of the meeting place!

PAUL'S RESPONSE

Against this bold breach of custom Paul urges four arguments. It will be helpful to examine each one.

1. *The secondary position of women* (1 Corin-

thians 11:3-9). As God has made it, human society—and even divine society—demonstrates a graded series of rank and order. Two men may be similar in many ways, but one may be an Army corporal and the other a lieutenant. A traffic policeman may be no intellectual or financial match for a corporation executive he tickets for speeding. Even though God and Christ are equal, there is a sense in which "the head of Christ is God" (11:3).

In the same way, women are naturally subordinate to men. It is important to distinguish *subordination* from *inferiority*. Subordination is a matter of rank, of organization. Inferiority is a matter of nature, of quality. What is subordinate is not necessarily inferior. Inferiority suggests an inner essential difference. But Paul is not saying women are inferior; he is saying they should be subordinate. And from here he goes on to urge continued use of the veil, the symbol of subordination.

To support this idea Paul goes to the Old Testament, as is often his practice. In a manner reflecting his training as a Jewish rabbi (Acts 22:3), Paul concludes the subordination of women from the facts that Eve was made for Adam, and not vice versa; that Adam was created first and then Eve; and that Eve was made from Adam's side (1 Corinthians 11: 8,9,12; compare Genesis 2:18-25).

2. *The angels.* "For this cause ought the woman to have power on her head because of the angels" (11:10). Phillips' version helps to clarify this difficult verse: "For this reason a woman ought to bear on her head an outward sign of man's authority for all the angels to see." But it is not certain just what Paul is thinking of here when he mentions "the angels." Some think he means guardian angels. Others think the reference may be to the lusting an-

gels of Genesis 6:1-4; going without the veil may tempt them. Recent scholars take the uncovered state as a possible insult to the angels, who were considered present with the worshipers.

3. *Nature itself.* "Doth not even nature itself teach you . . . ?" (1 Corinthians 11:14). We have a natural feeling that there is something not right about men having extremely long hair or women discarding proper symbols of subordination.

4. *The prevailing custom* (11:16). If these arguments are not enough to persuade the women at Corinth, they should recognize that the wearing of veils is the existing practice in the churches. By flouting this custom, they therefore threaten the unity of the church and aggravate the division of the Corinthian assembly.

SUBORDINATION IS NOT INFERIORITY

Women, however, stand equal to men before God. The letter of Paul to the Galatians was probably written some years before 1 Corinthians. Whether or not the ladies of Corinth had read it, they doubtless had at some time or other heard Paul preach (during his year and a half at Corinth) the same doctrine he described in Galatians 3:28: "There is neither Jew nor Greek, there is neither bond nor free, there is neither male nor female: for ye are all one in Christ Jesus."

If male and female distinctions are abolished in the church, how can Paul urge subordination? This is due to the necessary distinction between subordination and inferiority discussed earlier. So, in the midst of this plea for the retention of the veil, the apostle is able to assert, "Nevertheless neither is the man without the woman, neither the woman without the man, in the Lord" (11:11). For just as the first woman was taken from the side of Adam, so every man comes from the womb of his mother (11:12). And God has made both male and female. So there is an essential equality, but also a proper subordination between man and woman.

The Authority of Custom

The customs of the churches constitute a proper limitation to Christian behavior. "But if any man seem to be contentious, we have no such custom, neither the churches of God" (11:16). "Any man" in this verse applies equally well to any woman, for the Greek word used is both masculine and feminine. So Paul ends his discussion with a reference to the existing practice in the churches—the churches he himself had founded in his missionary efforts.

This is a remarkable verse, for it shows that Paul considered the standards set in the churches as a suitable guide to behavior. Such a standard was the recommendation of remaining as one was, rather than seeking either marriage or separation, which Paul says he ordains "in all the churches" (7:17). Peaceful worship, and not a noisy tumult, is the rule "in all churches of the saints" (14:33). When Timothy would come to Corinth he would, as Paul promises the Corinthians, "bring you into remembrance of my ways which be in Christ, as I teach every where in every church" (4:17). All Paul wanted of the Corinthians was that they respect the rules for behavior he commonly taught in all the churches.

But Paul was a man of special authority. He delivered to the Corinthians what he had ultimately received from Christ (11:23; 15:3); he referred to commands of the Lord (7:10; 14:37). Yet he offered advice for which he knew of no command (7:6,25), sealing his words with the statement that his judgment was tempered by his possession of the Holy Spirit (7:40).

Unfortunately, we do not have the apostle Paul in our own churches today to set standards for behavior. It might be helpful if we did. But we do have his writings. And the principles they expound are ever valid. It is entirely proper for local churches or denominations to decide upon customs regulating the social behavior of members and to expect general conformity.

ABUSE OF THE LORD'S SUPPER

The Lord's Supper in the Early Church was at first observed in connection with a fellowship meal. The Lord's Supper was instituted by Jesus at the Last Supper, which was itself a true meal (Mark 14:18,22; 1 Corinthians 11:25). The first-century practice of having frequent common meals has been discussed in the previous chapter. In Acts 2:42,46; 20:7 the common meals of the Christians are referred to as "the breaking of bread"—a common Jewish expression for eating (Acts 27:35; Lamentations 4:4). Distinctly Christian fellowship meals where the Lord's Supper was also observed came to be called "Love Feasts" (sometimes called "Agape Feasts," after the Greek word for love). Such love feasts are mentioned in Jude 12 and 2 Peter 2:13, where (as at Corinth) the meals were attended by unworthy persons. In time the ordinance of the Lord's Supper was detached from the common meals, possibly because of the dim view of common meals held by the Roman government.

At Corinth certain wealthy persons selfishly banded into cliques during the meal at which the Lord's Supper was observed. Such observance worked their own harm (1 Corinthians 11:17,27).

And it was not the *Lord's* supper they were convening (11:20). At such meals it was a common practice for each participant to bring some dish of food. Then all would share. But apparently the more wealthy were rushing ahead of the others, denying the poorer believers a share in their abundant foodstuffs. The result was that while some actually remained hungry, others became drunken. In such a situation, how could the Lord's Supper properly be held? They were partaking the Lord's Supper unworthily. We should observe that it was precisely this specific situation that prompted Paul's words about the Lord's Supper.

Paul urges the offenders to hold to the tradition he had relayed from Christ. "For I have received of the Lord that which also I delivered unto you . . ." (11:23). It was not Paul's command, but the Lord's, that they had so corrupted. He reminds them that this sacred act looks both backward (in remembrance of the Lord's death, 11:24,25) and forward (anticipating the Lord's return, 11:26).

Sharing in the Lord's Supper unworthily may actually result in judgment. To such indiscreet observance Paul attributed the many sicknesses at Corinth (11:30). Some had even died.

What does it mean to partake of the Lord's Supper unworthily? We see clearly what it meant for the Corinthians; they were doing it while guilty of selfishness, gluttony, drunkenness, and arrogance. This did not permit them to be aware of the sacred significance of the emblems of the bread and the wine; they were not discerning the Lord's body (11:29).

Christians are to share in the Lord's Supper in a mood of self-examination. Such self-judgment eliminates the need for the Lord's judgment. But when the Lord does judge, or chasten us, it is so we may escape the future judgment. It is in the light of this passage that we may come to understand the great principle presented in 1 Peter 4:12-19 and expressed in the words "judgment must begin at the house of God."

Both Jesus (in cleansing the temple) and Martin Luther (in beginning Protestantism) broke religious customs. There is a time to keep and a time to break custom. Customs must be kept and customs must be broken both on the single principle—whatever results in the glory of God and the profit of men (10:31 to 11:1).

7

The Etiquette of Spiritual Worship

Read 1 Corinthians 12-14

Etiquette, according to the latest Webster's unabridged dictionary, consists in "the rules of conduct, action, or pactice binding on members of a profession (as medicine or law), especially in their relations with one another." For the members of the body of Christ, assembled together in public worship, there are also rules of etiquette.

At the Corinthian assembly these rules were boldly and habitually disregarded. We have already seen how some of their women were overthrowing customs of dress, and how their observances of the common meal had disgraced the Lord's Supper. In 1 Corinthians 12 through 14 we learn that even in the use of the gifts of the Spirit true humility and even common courtesy were brushed aside. Because of the attention they received and of the honor they hoped to secure, certain members of this church were making a parade of their ability to speak in other tongues. In a community where excellence in oratory was cherished, the ability to speak ecstatically under the Holy Spirit's influence would have been highly prized. Selfish motives had corrupted a sacred blessing. Having begun in the Spirit, they were continuing in the flesh (Galatians 3:3).

Paul urges his errant infant church toward the unity characteristic of the body of Christ. They must renounce selfishness, replacing it with the most enduring gift of all—love. And loving consideration for others will restore order within the confused congregation.

RULE ONE: UNITY (1 CORINTHIANS 12)

There are true and false spiritual manifestations. The Holy Spirit is not the only spirit in the world. There are evil spirits as well. And Paul opens his treatment of spiritual gifts with a reminder to the Corinthians of their former state—a contrast Paul often draws (as in 6:11). They had been carried off to speechless idols that were worthless in themselves but mysteriously beset by evil spirits (10:20, 21). They had no doubt heard the ecstatic, unintelligible utterances spoken by the worshipers of numerous Greek gods. But now Paul will explain the vocal utterances prompted by the true God. Since He is living, He can speak. And by His Spirit He speaks to the church through the spiritual gifts.

No one moved by the true Spirit of God will ever curse Jesus. In the Hebrew synagogues of the day, curses were pronounced on heretics by the Jews, who were also taught to curse Jesus. On the other hand, it takes the Holy Spirit to genuinely acknowledge the Lordship of Jesus.

The gifts of the Holy Spirit are both many and varied. It is possible that our concept of the "gifts of the Spirit" is too limited. When Paul enumerates nine such gifts in 12:8-10 he does not say nor imply that these are all the ways in which the Spirit specially endows men. Within the same chapter (12:28) he lists other offices and operations along with some previously itemized in the ninefold list. In both 12:9 and 12:28 "gifts of healing" is in the plural—there are more than one. In 7:7, discussing marriage and staying single, Paul says every man has his proper *gift*—using exactly the same word he uses in these chapters for spiritual gifts. This means that we should allow God by His Spirit the privilege of accomplishing some things beyond what we may ask or think. His Spirit always moves in surprising ways.

But we have these several workings of the Holy Spirit listed as samples of His special endowments.

UNITY AND DIVERSITY IN THE BODY

Writers of the ancient world, even before Paul's time, were struck by the parallel between the marvelous human body and the structure of human society. After all, God had made both. But it was Paul who took this figure and applied it with such clarity to the body of Christ. As the human body consists of many parts and yet functions as a unit, so the body of Christ blends diversely gifted people into a single living organism. Not only in 1 Corinthians 12 is the illustration utilized by Paul. It is found also in Romans (12:5), Ephesians (1:22,23 and other places), and Colossians (1:18,24, and other places). In the latter two letters Christ is disclosed as the Head of His body, the Church. If the Church functions as does a living body, it will show unity through diversity. But the Corinthians had so distorted diversity into division that congregational unity was seriously imperiled, if not already fractured.

The lesson of the human body teaches another important truth. It is natural that some parts of the body will be more visible than others. But importance is never gauged by visibility. Certain tiny glands in the human body, never seen by ourselves or others, are absolutely essential to the body's healthy operation. And numerous obscure saints have exercised what gifts they had and thereby preserved the body of Christ.

Paul says that each member of the body cannot expect either to be the whole body or to do away with the other members (12:19-21,29,30). This suggests that we should not think we are to have all the spiritual gifts there are. Paul does say, "Covet earnestly the best gifts" (12:31), but he nowhere says covet all of them. In some groups today much is made of attempting to acquire all the gifts for each member. Just as logical would be a human body in which each finger also had eyes, feet, and internal organs! The unity of the body is made up by each member of the body being himself, having and exercising his own gift, rather than by each one trying to become the whole body (1 Peter 4:10,11).

THE SOVEREIGNTY OF THE SPIRIT

The gifts of the Spirit are given according to the Spirit's will. "But all these worketh that one and the selfsame Spirit, dividing to every man severally as he will" (12:11). It is the mind of the Holy Spirit that decides who gets which gift—and when. Observe Hebrews 2:4: God bore the first preachers witness through miraculous "gifts of the Holy Ghost, according to his own will." They spoke in tongues on the Day of Pentecost only so long "as the Spirit gave them utterance" (Acts 2:4). Notice how the Spirit is the origin of each of the gifts described in 1 Corinthians 12:8-11. All this means that there is a divine choice exercised in the matter of spiritual gifts. Two practical questions are often asked.

Do Christians possess the gifts or do the gifts possess the Christians? Is some one gift regularly manifested in the same believer, or should he look for any or all of them? The fact that Paul could speak of interpreters and prophets (14:28,29) suggests that persons are regularly endowed with such gifts. There is truth in both views, but the important thing is the sovereignty of the Spirit.

Can one receive the gifts of the Spirit without having received the baptism in the Spirit? This question is not directly answered in the Scriptures, and we may therefore be suspicious of the question. It implies a separation between initial and continuing work of the Holy Spirit—a separation to which apply also the words, "What God hath joined together let not man put asunder." One who thinks he has either the baptism in the Spirit or the gift(s) of the Spirit, without having the other, should reassess his Christian experience.

RULE TWO: LOVE (1 CORINTHIANS 13)

This chapter is one of the best known and best loved of the entire Bible. It is no accident that the great love chapter falls in the section on spiritual gifts. It belongs there. It is a part of what Paul advises to correct the Corinthian extremes. If their manifestations had been done in love for one another, then he may not have had to write this letter. Love is the rudder by which the gifts of the Spirit must be steered.

Love excels spiritual gifts. Several operations of the Holy Spirit are listed in 13:1,2. Then the startling statement is made that without love these spectacular occurrences dwindle to nothing at all. If a man's soul is worth more than the whole world, then love is worth more than all the gifts put together. For what is a gift if it is not used to uplift those witnessing its operation?

Love outlasts spiritual gifts. Paul singles out three gifts of the Spirit (13:8), then says that great as these are they will not endure. Prophecies, knowledge, tongues—all will eventually pass away. Yet love will endure, will outlast them all.

In short, love is greater in quality and longer in endurance than spiritual gifts. For this reason, it must control their expression. It is a most important rule of spiritual etiquette.

Rule Three: Upbuilding (1 Corinthians 14)

Taken from 1 Corinthians 14, here are some guidelines for courteously exercising the vocal gifts of the Spirit:

1. *The chief test and aim of any spiritual manifestation is edification,* or *upbuilding.* Edification means being built up, strengthened, confirmed. Eating in an idol temple is wrong since it might "embolden" (1 Corinthians 8:10, the same word translated "edify" in 1 Corinthians 14:4) the conscience of the weaker brother, that is, stimulate it to imitate the idol banqueting. Whatever happens—recalling Paul's rule in 10:31 to 11:1, of which this is merely an application—must be done in a way that will build up the participants and observers.

2. *Prophecy is superior to tongues.* This is the theme of 1 Corinthians 14:1-12. What is prophecy here? Either inspired utterance in the vernacular or possibly an element in anointed preaching. In 14:7-11 Paul illustrates from the fields of music, military strategy, and languages. In each case what is offered has to be distinct to be understood. Prophecy is better than tongues simply because it uses the hearer's language. A speaker in tongues, on the other hand, speaks to God alone. Since edification is the goal, and since tongues only edify the speaker, they should not be used in group worship. But there is a big exception.

3. *Interpreted tongues can contribute to uplifting*

worship. There is a public (14:22, 26-28; Acts 2:5-8) and a private (14:2,4,14,15,28) use for tongues. The public use of tongues demands interpretation; in private, one may speak mysteries to God letting his spirit pray (14:2,14,15; Romans 8:26,27). There is a special sign value to interpreted tongues in the presence of unbelievers (14:22). When an interpretation is provided for tongues, the same edifying effect as prophecy is secured. But in addition, there is the attractive feature of the tongues themselves.

4. *Improper spiritual manifestations can repel people from the church.* This might happen, Paul surmises (14:23), if everybody is speaking in tongues and no interpretation is provided. So he limits the number of such messages (14:27,28). If the unbeliever is to be profited or built up, he must hear a message he understands—either in the commonly used language (14:24,25) or in his own native tongue miraculously given (Acts 2:8,11). But God's method is always one of decent order rather than one of distressing confusion (14:33,40).

5. *"The spirits of the prophets are subject to the prophets"* (14:32). When the Holy Spirit convicts of sin, He can be resisted. It is possible to "quench" the Spirit (1 Thessalonians 5:19). Similarly, the one in whom the Spirit works has some degree of control over his manifestations. Since this is so, Paul can advise the speaker in tongues to refrain from speaking in the absence of an interpreter (14:28) and Paul does not consider this quenching the Spirit. Learning to cooperate with the Spirit involves risk of error—a risk any church takes when it encourages the operations of the Spirit. Had it not been for the errors of the Corinthians, we would have no letter from Paul to them. Paul's letters are of such eminent

use to us whose problems so often parallel those of the Corinthian church.

Thus, living unity wrought through love and issuing a mutual upbuilding displays the simple etiquette of spiritual worship.

BACKGROUND NOTE

A pagan example of ecstatic speech is found at Delphi to the north of Corinth. In this city was a famed oracle, a temple to which great and small came to seek guidance. After paying the required fee and performing the stipulated ceremonial rites, each inquirer was led into a room where he would be within hearing of a priestess. This priestess would perch on a tripod and, after being worked up into a frenzied state, would utter unintelligible words. The words were then allegedly interpreted by officiating priests and written out for the inquirer. Matters as small as business deals or as large as going to war with a neighboring country were presented to the oracle.

While the oracle was waning in popularity during the first century, it does show that utterances physically similar to speaking in tongues but produced other than by the Holy Spirit flourished even in that time. The many travelers passing through Corinth could have easily given firsthand accounts of this phenomenon. And it is possible that this may have contributed to the unwholesome attraction at Corinth to inspire utterance in unfamiliar speech. Paul then had to call to their attention the superiority of prophecy and the necessity of interpretation.

8

The More Excellent Way

Read 1 Corinthians 13

The German philosopher Schopenhauer tells a story about porcupines that illustrates the difficulties of manifesting Christian love in the touchy area of human relations. It seems the porcupines were cold during winter's blast, so they huddled together. But the closer they got the more they pricked each other with their sharp quills. But if they separated, they suffered from the cold. Christians need each other, but associations together are sometimes painful.

Love is more than one of the rules of spiritual worship. It is *The Greatest Thing in the World,* as Henry Drummond entitled his popular study of this chapter. No Christian virtue, no spiritual gift, excels God's love in us.

First Corinthians 13 is probably the best-known chapter in the New Testament. No survey of English literature would omit the King James Version of this chapter, so striking is its literary quality.

Nearly everyone knows that the word *charity* appearing throughout this chapter really means "love." The word *charity* has changed in meaning since the more than 350 years when the King James was prepared in A.D. 1611. This fact illustrates the usefulness of translations using today's language.

The poetic arrangement of phrases and the balance of structure in 1 Corinthians 13 are noteworthy. Scholars have made the intelligent guess that this passage became an early Christian hymn. Poets in the ancient world were less interested in rhyme than we are, and much more concerned about progress in thought and overall proportion.

Three stanzas, or sections, are commonly recognized. These embrace verses 1 to 3, 4 to 7, and 8 to 13. There are any number of ways to label these sections. You yourself may discover a fresh one. G. Campbell Morgan, one of the most widely known Bible teachers of a past generation and certainly one of the clearest outliners, called these divisions respectively the values, the virtues, and the victories of love. Henry Drummond spoke of the contrast, the analysis, and the defense of love.

In the first stanza (vv. 1-3) Paul itemizes seven things to which love—if a choice has to be made—is superior. In the second stanza (vv. 4-7) he lists 14 or 15 (depending on whether verse 6 is counted as one or two) characteristics of love. In the third stanza (vv. 8-13) the apostle shows that love outlasts spiritual gifts and outranks Christian virtues. Few Biblical passages fall into such neat and evident parts.

It is interesting to compare this description of love with that of wisdom given in Proverbs 8:1 to 9:12.

LOVE'S EXCELLENCE

It is easy to see the parallel form of these verses. Paul is saying that possessing the highest spiritual gifts gets a man no advantage if he does so without love. It is the mention of specific gifts—tongues, prophecy, knowledge, faith—which ties this chapter so securely to the preceding chapter. For he had just named these among the endowments distributed by the Spirit (12:8-10). And we know from Paul's words of correction in chapter 14 that it was abuse of the gift of tongues that called forth this whole section from the pen of the apostle.

1. *Tongues.* Inspired utterance in an unfamiliar language might take the form of a known but unlearned language (as on the Day of Pentecost). Or it might be a language no man understands (14:2).

But what are the tongues of angels? A Jewish writing from the first century before Christ bears the title *Testament of Job*, though it was not written by Job nor was it ever recognized as sacred literature by the Jews. This writing tells a fanciful story, typical of many developed by the Jewish rabbis as they built their "traditions of the elders." Just before his death Job gave each of his daughters a magical belt. When each in turn put on her belt, she spoke "in the language of the angels." Having been trained as a Jewish rabbi, Paul may have been acquainted with this writing. He is not specifically stating here that angels do have some special language. But he is saying that if they do, and if he would ever speak in such a language—and be without love—he would be nothing. Paul was once caught up into the third heaven and "heard unspeakable words which is not lawful for a man to utter" (2 Corinthians 12:4).

2. *Prophecy.* Here is the gift that Paul himself prefers to uninterpreted tongues in an assembly (14:5,19). But even this gift, with its vast value for the whole gathered church, is nothing without love. But is it possible to prophesy, to speak with inspiration, without love? For the answer to this we

71

need only recall the words of Jesus—one of the starkest passages of Scripture: "Many will say to me in that day, Lord, Lord, have we not prophesied in thy name? and in thy name have cast out devils? and in thy name done many wonderful works? And then will I profess unto them, I never knew you: depart from me, ye that work iniquity" (Matthew 7:22,23).

3. *Understanding mysteries.* Possibly this phrase goes with the following one. But Paul often spoke of knowing mysteries—his writings contain the word 21 times. In the very next section of this letter he speaks of the mystery of the transformation of believers at the Second Coming (15:51). (See also Romans 16:25,26.)

4. *Understanding all knowledge.* The spiritual gift discloses the "word of knowledge," that is, a specific bit of knowledge. Paul here suggests the unlikely possibility (in the light of 1 Corinthians 13:9-12) of possessing unlimited knowledge. But what he said earlier is true: "Knowledge puffs up; love builds up" (8:2, the way the Greek reads).

5. *Having all faith.* "If ye have faith as a grain of mustard seed," Jesus had said, "ye shall say unto this mountain, Remove hence to yonder place; and it shall remove: and nothing shall be impossible unto you" (Matthew 17:20). Love excels mountain-moving!

6. *Philanthropy.* Verse 3 shows a progression; neither giving one's goods nor oneself has any significance apart from love. The custom referred to here is the common Jewish one of almsgiving. Jesus even gave instructions for almsgiving (Matthew 6:1-4), in which we learn that trumpet-blaring pride had quenched the motive of love for some almsgivers. The apostle Barnabas, one of Paul's earlier associates, had

given his property to the church (Acts 4:36,37), doubtless from pure motives. The tragedy of Ananias and Sapphira is contrasted with the benefits of Barnabas and shows loveless philanthropy (Acts 5:1-11).

7. *Martyrdom.* Even the ultimate sacrifice, death itself, is meaningless without love. In Athens, Paul probably saw the monument that had been set up by a gentleman from India in honor of himself after he had ignited himself on a pyre. Paul knew the story of the three Hebrew children who escaped martyrdom in the fiery furnace (Daniel 3). Not too many years hence Christians would be ignited to furnish illumination in the Roman arena. Yet sacrificial death without love is worthless.

Love—the love of God shed abroad in our hearts by the Spirit of God—is what validates all spiritual gifts, all Christian virtues.

LOVE'S NATURE

The characteristics of love are detailed in this chapter. Love is:

1. *Patient.* Patience is the willingness to wait. The Greek word is made up from two words meaning something like "far from deep wrath." "Slow to anger" is another way of putting it. "Be patient toward all men," the apostle elsewhere advised (1 Thessalonians 5:14). Barclay observes that in the New Testament the word always speaks of patience with people, not with circumstances. Patience is a characteristic of God himself (Romans 2:4; 1 Peter 3:20).

2. *Kindly.* Love shows a down-to-earth goodness; it "looks for a way of being constructive," as Phillips translates. From the description of the way in which the Corinthians observed their love feasts (1 Corinthians 11:17-22), it appears that they were anything

73

but kind toward one another. Ask yourself how you would treat a convicted prostitute. Then see how Jesus manifested supreme kindness in John 8:1-11.

3. *Not jealous.* If any assembly in the first century was torn by envy it was Corinth. Perilous divisions had split up their congregation into petty cliques. Paul could not address them as mature believers because of their squabbles (1 Corinthians 3:3). Love could mend schisms in the body (12:25). This item begins a series of eight negative characteristics of love.

4. *Not boastful.* The word used appears only here in the New Testament and is rare in Greek anywhere. It comes from a noun meaning a braggart, and is therefore quite close in meaning to the following.

5. *Not puffed up.* This and the previous phrase Phillips renders, "neither anxious to impress nor does it cherish inflated ideas of its own importance." Surprisingly, the Corinthians were puffed up even over the case of unmentionable immorality in their midst (5:2,6). Those who prided themselves on their higher notions about the insignificance of idols were the recipients of Paul's caution that "knowledge puffeth up" (8:1). As we observed in an earlier chapter, unwise glorying (boasting) is frequently rebuffed in 1 Corinthians (1:29; 3:18,21; 4:6,7; 5:2,6; 8:1; 14:37). Good advice: "He that glorieth, let him glory in the Lord" (1:31).

6. *Not ill-mannered.* The word means not behaving according to the scheme of things. A related word, roughly translated "well-schemed," is used in 14:40, where Paul pleads that things be done decently. Even their manners at worship services needed attention!

7. *Not selfish.* Barclay says, "does not insist on

its rights"—an apt phrase for the Corinthian ladies who wished to relinquish wearing the veil! Not about property, but about interests, does Paul elsewhere advise, "Look not every man on his own things, but every man also on the things of others" (Philippians 2:4). (See also 1 Corinthians 10:24.)

8. *Not quick-tempered.* Anger has various ways of expressing itself. Some who successfully control outbursts, conceal smoldering wrath within. Phillips' rendering makes us all guilty: "not touchy." It may well be that Paul speaks here from an indelible lesson learned in his earlier dispute with Barnabas (Acts 15:39).

9. *Not retaliatory.* This is a quotation from Zechariah 8:17, the only Old Testament quotation in the passage. The word comes from the field of business, where it is used of keeping accounts. So Paul is saying love does not record every ill received for later retaliation. The King James phrase, "thinketh no evil," sometimes leads to a misconception well corrected by one commentator: "It is hardly necessary to point out how far removed indiscriminating trust is from the teaching of the apostle Paul, and from that of the entire New Testament, by which a healthy mistrust is recommended of all false prophets, 'wolves,' 'dogs,' 'foxes,' and, in general, of all the wiles of Satan and hordes."

10. *Not gloating.* Love takes no pleasure in hearing bad things of another. Its source of joy is not the wickedness of others. This is the last of the eight negative characteristics.

11. *Truth-loving.* Love's joy comes from sharing in truth—not, as the other part of verse 7 says, in unrighteousness. Note that the opposite of iniquity is considered to be truth.

12. *Forever forbearing.* The "all things" in this

75

set of four similarly constructed characteristics found in verse 7, may very well mean rather "at all times." There is some repetition of ideas in this lengthy list.

13. *Forever trustful.* "Believeth all things" needs the caution observed under number 9 above. Check other translations.

14. *Forever hopeful.* There is "no fading of its hope" (Phillips).

15. *Forever patient.* Different words, but the same idea, thus open and close the list.

It is love of this quality, realized only in the deeper work of the Holy Spirit, which the Corinthians—and we—need. We must not forget that love of this sort is a fruit of the Spirit (Galatians 5:22). Magnanimous acts done without this specific quality of love do not come within the apostle's thought.

LOVE'S PERMANENCE

Tongues shall pass away—these are the apostle's words. And so will knowledge and even prophecies. He thus isolates three gifts and says love will outlast them all. When will the gifts pass away, having served their purpose? The presence of knowledge in the group forbids the common interpretation that the gifts of the Spirit ceased at the end of the Apostolic Era. In fact, it is not a historically accurate statement to affirm that the gifts have ever ceased. They will have served their purpose when the "perfect" comes. A clew to when this is arises from a look at 1 Corinthians 15:24-28. The future return of Jesus will trigger a chain of last-time events that will witness the remaking of human society and the culmination of all things in the kingdom of God.

Till then, Paul says, our knowledge is partial—and even our prophesying is "in part." Despite the presence in this age of spiritual gifts, our knowledge will not be perfected until later.

So faith, hope, and love will outlast the gifts of the Spirit. It is well worth noting that this means then that the fruit of the Spirit will outlast the gifts of the Spirit. The Corinthians needed this message. And today's Christians can use it as well.

9

Destroying the Last Enemy

Read 1 Corinthians 15; 2 Corinthians 5:1-10

Evangelist Dwight L. Moody, who died in 1899, once said the following: "Someday you will hear that Dwight L. Moody is dead. Don't believe it, for in that moment I shall be more alive than ever."

To the world surrounding the Corinthian church, the Christian doctrine of the resurrection was something of a novelty. If it was believed at all, it was construed in vague or mythical terms. Often ideas of the rebirth of life were connected with the course of the four seasons: every springtime the fruitless branches and the barren fields suddenly sprouted green shoots. In Egypt, in Babylonia, in Greece, and elsewhere elaborate fanciful tales sprang up about gods who came to life again with each new spring. These tales form a major theme of ancient mythology.

But if there was one thing central to the earliest Christian preaching, it was the resurrection of Christ. Scholars who have studied the sermons of Acts have noted that early teachings uniformly make a point out of the miraculous resurrection of Christ. In fact, what the Exodus is to the Old Testament the resurrection of Christ is to the New Testament. Each is the standard of God's miraculous power.

In this chapter we see once again how pagan ideas

beset the church. The church was in the world; but, alas! the world was in the church.

"The last enemy that shall be destroyed," said the apostle Paul, "is death." The sting is taken out of death, its fear conquered, by the Christian gospel. At the heart of that gospel is the good news that man need not die—a fact already previewed by Enoch and Elijah. The believer who has died in the Lord, as well as he who is alive at the Lord's return, looks forward to a gloriously new "spiritual body." For those who have died in the Lord, this comes by resurrection; for the others, through miraculous change. But the guarantee of both is the resurrection of Christ.

RESURRECTION DENIED

The ancient world deeply pondered the future life. Man has always wondered what life is like—or if there is any life—after death. Beliefs about the future of human existence that were current at the time the Corinthian assembly was flourishing include the following:

1. *Fanciful myths.* Vague notions that the dead lived on in their tombs prompted such acts as burial of household objects with the bodies or continued attention paid the dead by the living. The gods of Greece and elsewhere were periodically reborn, often in connection with the revival of nature in spring.

2. *Extinction.* The Epicureans taught that man is composed of atomic particles which dissolve at death. Therefore, human existence terminates with death. (Compare Acts 7:18,32.)

3. *Absorption.* The Stoics believed that every man housed a bit of the fiery spirit that was their idea of God. (See Acts 17:18,32.) After death, while the

body disintegrated, this fiery spirit returned to the divine nature and was reabsorbed into it. In effect, this belief also terminates individual existence.

4. *Immortality of the soul.* Especially popularized by the great Greek philosopher Plato, the Greeks generally believed that the soul was good but the body, since it was made of matter, was evil. The body would decay at death, but the soul would live on.

5. *Resurrection of the same physical body.* Full understanding of the resurrection from the dead awaited the revelation of the New Testament and its Lord, and this is one illustration of the progressive character of revelation. Not much is said of the resurrection in the Old Testament. Some texts gloomily anticipate the grave (Psalms 6:5; 30:9; 88:10-12; 115:17; Isaiah 38:18). But there are glimpses of a coming resurrection (Job 19:25-27; Daniel 12:2). And Jesus said Moses knew of the resurrection, else he would not have spoken of God as the God of Abraham, Isaac, and Jacob—who were living people, as God is not the God of the dead but of the living (Matthew 22:31-33).

Unlike the Greeks who thought of the body as evil, the Hebrews had a healthy appreciation of the human body. For them it was holy, the gift of God and the work of His creation (Psalm 139:14). The Jews stressed man as an inidividual, and they consequently thought of the resurrection as naturally involving the body each man had received from the Creator. But, as we are about to see, Paul showed that the resurrection body would not be the same as this present body, but a new one clothed with glory and honor.

Thus in the world surrounding the Corinthian church, the Christian teaching of the resurrection, so central to the whole Christian gospel (15:1-5), would be a striking novelty. It is easy to see why, as Paul preached at Mars' Hill, "when they heard of the resurrection of the dead, some mocked: and others said, We will hear thee again of this matter" (Acts 17:32). Mars' Hill, at Athens, was hardly 50 miles from Corinth. And there were even some Jews, the Sadducees, who denied the resurrection (Acts 23:8).

This background helps us understand why Paul wrote his letter to answer those among the Corinthians who were saying, "There is no resurrection of the dead" (15:12).

Denying the resurrection is illogical. The Corinthian heretics were not saying Christ had not arisen. Their contention was a more general one: they simply affirmed that men do not rise from the dead. Paul took up this faulty premise and showed how it would lead to several unacceptable conclusions. If there is no resurrection from the dead, then—

1. *Christ has not arisen* (15:13,16). See how clearly Paul classifies Christ as a human being. If men do not arise from the dead, then Christ—also a man —did not arise. Of course this does not keep Paul from elsewhere stressing the divine nature of Christ (Phillipians 2:6-11).

2. *The Corinthians have believed in vain* (15:14, 17,19). Regeneration is impossible without the resurrection.

3. *Corinthians who have died in the Lord are lost* (15:18). Apart from the hope of the resurrection, the Christian dead are as lost as are the non-Christian dead.

4. *Paul preached lies* (15:14,15). Since he proclaimed the Resurrection, he lied—if indeed there is

no resurrection of the dead. Since his opponents were not likely to accept these conclusions, Paul thus shows the foolishness of a premise which logically leads to them.

RESURRECTION AFFIRMED

The Resurrection was a central part of early Christian preaching. This is seen clearly by studying the contexts (all are sermons) of Acts 2:24,32; 3:15,26; 4:10; 5:30; 10:40; 13:30. In each one of these references mention is made of the resurrection of Christ.

In the 20 years or so between the ascension of Christ and when the earliest books of the New Testament began to appear, the gospel was passed on orally. To guard against alteration it took on fixed forms; that is, though each preacher used his own personality there was a fixed body of truth which all proclaimed. It is to this body of truth that Paul refers in 1 Corinthians 15:1-7. He received it; he passed it on to the Corinthians. He praised them for keeping these "ordinances," these traditions (11:2). In 2 Thessalonians 2:15 and 3:6, passages written before the Corinthian letters, we find Paul urging retention of these specific principles. At the heart of this crystallized body of teaching lay the resurrection of Christ, that miraculous deed of God which so powerfully energizes the whole Christian faith.

Christ's resurrection is the first of a series. His resurrection is termed the "firstfruits of them that slept." This word goes back to Leviticus 23:10,11. The harvest of a crop could not be used or sold until a portion was dedicated to the Lord. Stephanus (1 Corinthians 16:15) was the "firstfruits of Achaia," that is, he was the first convert in the province of which Corinth was the capital. Glorious as it is, our possession of the Spirit is but the "firstfruits"—merely a foretaste of what is to come (Romans 8:23). So Christ's resurrection was the first real resurrection. Because of Christ's resurrection, all other and subsequent resurrections are guaranteed.

(Three times Jesus miraculously brought people back from the dead: a. the daughter of Jairus [Mark 5:22-43]; b. the widow's son [Luke 7:11-17]; c. Lazarus [John 11:38-44]. But these miracles were not strictly resurrections: they were restorations of natural life. The same bodies again came to life. Such miracles show Jesus has power over death. Enoch and Elijah escaped death and went dircetly into God's presence. But only Jesus truly died and was miraculously resurrected into that new and to us somewhat mysterious body of the Resurrection.)

Verses 24 to 28 of 1 Corinthians 15 speak of the final end of all things, when the kingdom of God reaches its fullest manifestation. This grand feat begins with the resurrection of Christ.

Resurrection Proved

There is something about "proof" and "argument" that is foreign to the field of faith. It is possible to be so taken up with proofs and arguments that the spirit of the matter, the heart of the issue slips through one's fingers. The kind of reasoning and proofs offered by the earliest Christian preachers was the sort that clears away mental difficulties thus preparing the way for faith. We must never think that God lies at the end of some argument. For intellectual reasoning is just one more variety of human wisdom, and as Paul had spelled out so clearly to the Corinthians earlier, "the wisdom of this world is foolishness with God" (3:19).

83

Still, there were several lines of evidence on the basis of which a confident belief in the reality of the Resurrection could be held. Paul showed that the Resurrection was proved—

1. *By attested witnesses.* It is worth noting all these witnesses are believers. Jesus does not now, as He did not then, show himself to those without belief. This does not mean He avoids those with sincere doubts, with difficulties to belief. For in Christ's appearances to the apostles, one appearance was especially convincing to "Doubting Thomas" (John 20:24-29). Saving faith is much more a matter of trustful and total commitment of oneself to a Person than of a hasty assent dishonestly concealing suppressed uncertainties.

2. *By personal revelation.* "He was seen of me also," said Paul recalling the scene described in Acts 9:1-9. Paul knew whereof he spoke.

3. *By believers' experience.* First Corinthians 15: 29-34 assembles several practices of believers that would be senseless if there were no resurrection. The first of these is the obscure practice (mentioned nowhere else in Scripture) of baptism for the dead (1 Corinthians 15:29). It appears that this practice, which never became a general one in the church, was a sort of proxy baptism. Without approving or disapproving it, Paul simply says why do it if the dead are not raised? And why, if there is no resurrection, does the apostle face the threat of death every day as he proclaims the gospel about the Mediterranean world? Neither his perilous preaching nor their proxy baptisms are of any use if there is no resurrection.

RESURRECTION EXPLAINED

"Flesh and blood cannot inherit the kingdom of

God" (15:50). "The kingdom of God is not meat and drink; but righteousness, and peace, and joy in the Holy Ghost" (Romans 14:17). In its full and final manifestation, the reign of God (another translation for "kingdom") will be without the presence of sin and the bodies sin has touched. All human bodies we know are those tainted with sin and therefore subject to corruption. But true human nature is found only in three places in the total scheme of redemption: in Adam before the Fall, in Jesus Christ, and in our future glorious resurrection bodies. We have never seen or felt what it is like to be normally human—that is, without sin—but this is our future.

The resurrection body is not this present body. This one is corruptible, dishonorable, weak, natural. That one is incorruptible, glorious, powerful, spiritual. A hint of its character comes from the nature of Jesus' resurrection body, which had characteristics of this present body (Luke 24:41-43) yet features unknown to us (Luke 24:31; John 20:19). Unlike the Greeks who immortalized the soul but did away with the body and unlike the Jews who looked for the same body revived, the Christians expect changed bodies. Theoretical questions about bodies tragically torn in accidents or scattered in ashes never occurred either to Paul or to his readers, so far as we are told. Paul did not expect this body to be reconstituted. He taught the survival of individuality, and each person would have the new body which, as to the seed, God gives "as it hath pleased him" (15:38).

RESURRECTION APPLIED

Very typically, Paul converts a mystery (15:51) into an exhortation (15:58). The Resurrection is no mere theological dogma laid to rest in some dusty volume. It is the keystone of the living Christian faith, the source of all Christian life. Because of the Resurrection, we know the Lord lives. Because He lives, we live. Because we live in the sunlight of resurrection power our work is sure and our future secure.

10

Stewards of Mysteries

Read 1 Corinthians 3, 4; 2 Corinthians 1-7

TRUSTEES

"Shall I enter the ministry?" asked a youth of an experienced minister. "Not if you can help it," was the wise reply. The minister knew that one called of God to the work of the Christian ministry cannot be ultimately happy in any other profession or calling. He did not mean that one divinely chosen would not personally prefer some other calling or could not be successful in any other. A man who would make a successful minister would be a likely success in many lines of work. But he meant that there is an irresistible magnestism of which the candidate is always conscious whether (as with Paul) this originated with an explosive encounter with Christ in a dramatic experience or (as with Timothy) "from a child" he knew the Scriptures which eventually led him into the ministry.

"Trustees of the secrets of God!" This, in the words of Phillips' translation, is how Paul wished the Corinthians to regard him and their other ministers. Ministers are agents—they do not represent themselves but Another. Their stock-in-trade is "the mysteries of God"—mysteries now unveiled by the open preaching of the gospel.

Second Corinthians is, above all other New Testament books, the book of the Christian minister. In it the heart of one of the greatest Christian preachers lies bared. It is one of the most personal, most intimate of books. It is not easy reading, for it is addressed to a congregation from its pastor and matters between them are somewhat private. Between its lines we detect unmistakable traces of stiff and unfair opposition to the great apostle. He writes gently, but he promises to be severe when necessary.

C. M. Ward once remarked that he finds reflected in 2 Corinthians every problem a modern minister has to face. Second Corinthians provides one of the best commentaries on 1 Corinthians 13. For the same Paul who there wrote of love now shows us that applied love is no milk-toast affair but demands harsh action when people remain unrepentant.

THE SECOND CORINTHIAN LETTER

Second Corinthians was written at least several months after 1 Corinthians, possibly late in the year A.D. 57. The letter was occasioned by the return of Titus from Corinth to Macedonia, to which Paul had come after leaving Ephesus (2 Corinthians 2: 12,13; 7:5-7,13). Titus brought good news about a change of heart among at least some of the Corinthians. Paul at this time wrote 2 Corinthians to prepare for his coming visit (2 Corinthians 2:14,20,21; 13:1,2,10).

There are three discernible divisions in 2 Corinthians, despite the intensely personal character of the letter. Chapters 1 to 7 express the apostle's reassurance over their altered behavior. They also disclose a loving appeal from the pastor to his people. Chapters 8 and 9 deal with a specific matter, the collection for the poor saints in Jerusalem. In chapters 10 to 13 Paul fiercely opposes his lingering enemies at Corinth, self-styled "apostles" who were enticing the Corinthians away from the pure gospel he had earlier preached to them. This personal defense forces Paul into reluctant boasting about his apostleship, his trials, even his intimate spiritual experiences.

VARIETIES OF THE MINISTRY

"Are all apostles? are all prophets? are all teachers?" (1 Corinthians 12:29). Thus Paul asked them, expecting negative answers, in the chapter on how variety is necessary to the unity of the body of Christ. One of the specific faults of the Corinthian congregation lay in their favoritism regarding ministers. And Paul concluded, in effect, that it was foolish to limit oneself to this or that minister when all were set in the Church by God for its edification (1 Corinthians 3:22).

It is a surprising revelation to discover just how many of the famous preachers of the New Testament had served the Corinthian congregation. Here is a list of those we are told were there at one time or another. There must have been others, also.

1. *Paul, the Founder.* The leading apostle to the Gentiles spent a year and a half with the Corinthians and was devoted to "teaching the word of God among them" (Acts 18:11). For all that, they still fell into the deep problems we read about in the Corinthian letters.

2. *Apollos, the "Waterer."* There is a beautiful thought in 1 Corinthians 3:6: "Apollos watered." He had the ministry of quenching spiritual thirst. Perhaps it was through the ministry of Apollos that Paul could say they had "been all made to drink into one Spirit" (1 Corinthians 12:13). Was Apollos qualified? Acts reports of him that he was "an eloquent man, and mighty in the Scriptures," "instructed in the way

89

of the Lord," and "fervent in the spirit" (Acts 18:24, 25). After he was further instructed in the ways of the Lord by that helpful lay couple, Aquila and Priscilla, he went to Achaia—the province of which Corinth was the capital. There he "helped them much which had believed through grace" (Acts 18:27). There are ministers today who, like Apollos, water God's farm (which is what "husbandry" in 1 Corinthians 3:9 means) with showers of spiritual blessing. It is understandable how an "Apollos party" could develop at Corinth.

3. *Timothy, the Reminder.* "For this cause," explained the apostle Paul in his first letter (1 Corinthians 4:17), "have I sent unto you Timotheus, who is my beloved son, and faithful in the Lord, who shall bring you into remembrance of my ways which be in Christ, as I teach every where in every church." This young understudy of the apostle had been of great use in establishing the Thessalonians (1 Thessalonians 3:1-3), and when Paul was about to send him to the Philippians he confided, "I have no man like-minded, who will naturally care for your state" (Philippians 2:20). Not only did the apostle address two letters to Timothy (1 and 2 Timothy), he also often included his name in letters that he himself wrote, as may be seen from the initial verses of 2 Corinthians, Philippians, 1 and 2 Thessalonians, and Philemon. Timothy must have been a sensitive youth, for Paul tells the Corinthians to see that his stay is without fear (1 Corinthians 16:10,11).

4. *Titus, the Fund Raiser.* Apparently a stronger personality than Timothy, Titus was received among the Corinthians "with fear and trembling" (2 Corinthians 7:15). Titus initiated the collection among the Corinthians for the poor saints in Jerusalem

(2 Corinthians 8:6). And Paul recommended Titus to them as "my partner and fellow helper concerning you" (2 Corinthians 8:23).

5. *Silas, the Exhorter.* Acts says Silas was of the "chief men among the brethren," a "prophet," and one who "exhorted the brethren with many words, and confirmed them" (Acts 15:22,32). From 2 Corinthians 1:19 we learn that Silas preached also at Corinth. (*Silvanus* is the form of the name used by Paul and Peter, while *Silas* is used in Acts.)

6. *Unnamed brethren.* In 2 Corinthians 8:18 and 22 Paul describes without naming the two men chosen to accompany Titus in relaying the funds. One was famous for his diligence. There are many unnoticed ministers today of equal qualifications.

7. *Helpful laymen.* What a fine service to the church was provided by those lay tentmakers, Aquila and Priscilla. Paul spoke of them as "my helpers in Christ Jesus" (Romans 16:3) and they were of use to the mighty Apollos, "whom when Aquila and Priscilla had heard, they took him unto them, and expounded unto him the way of God more perfectly" (Acts 18:26). Stephanas and his house had "addicted themselves to the ministry of the saints" (1 Corinthians 16:15). Months later, Gaius hosted, not only Paul, but the whole church while Paul was in Corinth (Romans 16:23).

It is sobering to realize that the Corinthian church could have been so beset with problems of every sort, having had this succession of ministers! The truth emerges that "God gave the increase" (1 Corinthians 3:6) and that even though it was the church "at Corinth" it was "the church of God" (1 Corinthians 1:2). Against this Church, Jesus promised,

"The gates of hell shall not prevail" (Matthew 16:18)

Vocabulary of the Ministry

What is the job of the minister? Two ways to answer this question are to look first at the titles given to ministers in the Corinthian letters and then to consider the words describing what ministers do.

TITLES FOR MINISTERS

1. *"Ministers of Christ"* (1 Corinthians 4:1). The word used means an assistant. In earlier Greek it referred to an under-rower who assisted the oarsmen.

2. *"Ministers of God"* (2 Corinthians 6:4; compare 2 Corinthians 3:6, where the same Greek word appears). Not the same Greek word as in the previous title, this is the word ordinarily translated "deacon" (1 Timothy 3:8) or "servant" (John 2:5; Romans 16:1). Not only was Timothy described as a "minister of God" (1 Thessalonians 3:2), but among Paul's opponents at Corinth were some ministers of Satan (2 Corinthians 11:15). So ministers are Christ's assistants and God's deacons!

3. *"Stewards of mysteries"* (1 Corinthians 4:1). A steward is a household business manager. Ministers oversee the secrets of God.

4. *"Labourers together with God"* (1 Corinthians 3:9; 2 Corinthians 6:1). Ministers are not the source, but the channel, of God's saving power. They have to learn to cooperate with Him—a task more easily said than done!

5. *"Messengers of the churches"* (2 Corinthians 8:23). This phrase uses the same word translated (as 1 Corinthians 1:1) "apostle," which always means one sent on a specific mission.

6. *"Ambassadors for Christ"* (2 Corinthians 5:20).

92

Ambassadors represent their government to a foreign nation. Ministers represent God to an alienated world. By extension, all Christians are Christ's ambassadors.

7. *"Your servants"* (2 Corinthians 4:5). *Slaves* is an alternate translation of this word. A ministry that is not service is not a ministry.

WORDS FOR MINISTERING

1. *"Preach."* One word for preaching means to present good news (1 Corinthians 1:17). Another means to proclaim widely (2 Corinthians 4:5). The first describes the contents, the second the method of preaching.

2. *"Speak"* (1 Corinthians 2:7). More restricted speaking, as in counseling, does much in the direct application of the gospel to those in need.

3. *"Deliver"* (1 Corinthians 15:3). The minister passes along what he has received from Christ and through the church.

4. *"Teach"* (Acts 18:11). Education, as well as evangelism and exhortation, makes up the work of the ministry. (See Matthew 28:19,20.)

5. *"Intreat"* (1 Corinthians 4:13). Persuasive pleading has its place in the effort to secure commitment, by whatever means.

6. *"Warn"* (1 Corinthians 4:14). Some who will not be entreated must be warned.

7. *"Testify"* (Acts 18:5). The word signifies testimony given under oath. The minister is a *witness* first and foremost.

8. *"Reason"* (Acts 18:4). Ministers present, not some formal, logical "proof" centered in human wisdom, but an intelligent discussion which clears the way for the arrival of faith.

TRIALS OF THE MINISTRY

No part of Scripture shows more clearly the problems ministers face than the Corinthian letters. First Corinthians vividly portrays the *church problems* a minister can expect to encounter; 2 Corinthians exemplifies his *personal problems*.

By now you can probably recall the details of the following problems at Corinth which have modern counterparts:

church cliques (1 Corinthians 1:10)
immorality (1 Corinthians 6:18)
immaturity (1 Corinthians 3:1)
doctrinal error (1 Corinthians 15:12)
marriage troubles (1 Corinthians 7:10)
abuse of spiritual gifts (1 Corinthians 14:23)
misused liberty (1 Corinthians 8:11)
custom-breaking (1 Corinthians 11:16)

Second Corinthians has to be read and reread to sense the pulse-beat of the great apostle. But we can find in the Corinthian letters evidence of the following personal trials any minister will face:

embarrassment (1 Corinthians 4:9-13)
discouragement (2 Corinthians 1:8; 7:6,7)
relinquished rights (1 Corinthians 9:12)
misunderstanding (2 Corinthians 11:7,8)
opposition (1 Corinthians 9:3; 2 Corinthians 10:10)

Facing problems is a minister's daily business. But if he follows Paul's example he will be in constant touch with the Lord of Glory who is the Source of all healing.

Support of the Ministry

How are ministers to be paid? There is a simple answer: their support should come from those to whom they minister. Such a pattern was—

1. *Instituted by God.* "Even so hath the Lord ordained that they which preach the gospel should

94

live of the gospel" (1 Corinthians 9:14). Even in the Law, God had the ox get his support from his service (1 Corinthians 9:8-10).

2. *Approved by Christ.* Ever wonder how Jesus supported himself during His years of earthly ministry? (See Luke 8:3 for the answer.) The commissioned disciples were to accept the support of their hosts (Luke 9:3-6).

3. *Practiced by Paul.* As discussed earlier in chapter 5, Paul probably relinquished the right to support at Corinth because of the attitude such a practice would have awakened there. But he took support from other churches (2 Corinthians 11:8) and the whole argument of 1 Corinthians 9:1-27 would make no sense if Paul did not think it just to expect ministerial support.

The church has an obligation to support its ministry. But the ministry has an even more urgent obligation to see that it does not become "greedy of filthy lucre" (1 Timothy 3:3).

REWARDS OF THE MINISTRY

Not much is said about what one gets from the ministry. The very idea of reward is opposite to selfless service. Still, to borrow again from Paul's example, there are two spheres in which the minister finds satisfaction for his service:

1. *The Growth of the Church.* The congregation is the minister's boast, in spite of their deficiencies and failures (2 Corinthians 7:4). The congregation alone recommends him to the church and the world (2 Corinthians 3:1-3). For them he gives God thanks (1 Corinthians 1:4). The minister knows that though he plants, another waters, it is God who causes growth.

2. *The Approval of God.* There is a reward for the minister who rightly builds (1 Corinthians 3:14). But it lies beyond this life and consists primarily in the approval of God, whom he here serves.

11

The New Agreement

Read 1 Corinthians 11:17-34; 2 Corinthians 2:12 to 4:6

"BEYOND THE SACRED PAGE . . ."

What is the New Testament? You are entitled to think such a question is an insult. Everyone knows, you will readily say, the New Testament is a book, the second half of the Holy Bible which Christians regard as their sacred Scriptures. And you are correct.

But this very book we call the New Testament speaks about a "new testament." When it mentions this "new testament" it is not speaking of a book as we do today. Instead, whenever our printed New Testaments (whether one of those tiny pocket New Testaments or the second part of your Bible) speak about the "new testament" they are referring to a brand-new covenant set up by Jesus which now governs our relationship with God. This covenant is called "new" because it is contrasted with the Law, the old way of being right before God—a way superseded by the mission of Jesus on the cross.

It is this idea of a new agreement between God and man that we find Paul using in 2 Corinthians, chapter 3. As we have already seen, Paul is earnestly defending his ministry before his detractors at Corinth. No doubt, they were Jews (2 Corinthians 11: 22). And here we find Paul, the converted Jew, saying how much more glorious a ministry he has than

Moses had, even though Moses' ministry was so bright that at one time he had to wear a veil. No wonder Paul sings praise to God who has made him and the other Corinthian ministers "competent administrators of the new agreement" (2 Corinthians 3:6, Phillips).

Once in 1 Corinthians (11:23-26) and once in 2 Corinthians (3:4-18) Paul speaks about the "new testament." The passages about the institution of the Lord's Supper in Matthew 26:28; Mark 14:24; and Luke 22:20 are parallel to 1 Corinthians 11:25. Elsewhere in the New Testament the idea of the new covenant is discussed, especially in Hebrews. (See Hebrews 7:22; 8:8-13; 9:1-20.)

Promised by the Prophets

God regularly governs his relations with men by a covenant. Any form of life, even in human society, demands some sort of common agreement on rules by which all will abide. This necessity lies at the basis of human law and governs action in communities, for example in families, where there is no written law.

As early as Adam and Eve in the Garden of Eden we find imposed the terms of a covenant (Genesis 1:28; 2:16,17; 3:14,15). God made a covenant with Noah (Genesis 9:8-17) and another with Abraham (Genesis 15:18). In fact, the history of the people of Israel is one of the establishment, renewal—and unfortunately, the breaking—of covenants. Thus the covenant was renewed under Joshua (Joshua 8:32-35), under King Josiah (2 Kings 23:3), under Ezra and Nehemiah (Nehemiah 8:2,3,18).

There is a beautiful chapter in Ezekiel 16 that will reward a careful reading. Written with the frankness of the eastern mind, it presents Israel in the figure of a habitually errant wife who had broken the covenant God had established in her youth (16:8). "Nevertheless," promises ever-faithful God, "I will remember my covenant with thee in the days of thy youth, and I will establish unto thee an everlasting covenant" (16:60). That is rather typical of all God's covenants: though man is unfaithful to his part, God remains true.

A covenant in the Biblical sense is not the same as a commercial agreement. A negotiated contract between labor and management of some industry is typical of modern covenants. Over the bargaining table, perhaps with the aid of mediators, representatives of the working man and of the capital investor state their demands. Through what is often a long process, sometimes interrupted by strikes or violence, an agreement is reached that is binding on both parties. Each may not have gained from the contract all he hoped to secure, but each agrees to abide by it.

But a covenant made with God is different. It is different because the parties are unequal. God is incomparably superior to man, so when any covenant exists between them it is always God's doing and on God's terms. The very fact that He would give a covenant at all is a manifestation of His grace. For this reason the Bible talks about God "establishing" a covenant (Genesis 9:9; Ezekiel 16:60) or "enjoining" one (Hebrews 9:20), rather than "coming to terms" as we might say.

THE BIBLICAL IDEA OF "COVENANTS"

The Hebrew and Greek words translated "covenant" or "testament" have several meanings.

1. *Will or testament.* Used in this sense, the word *covenant* refers to a legal document expressing the

desire of a person as to what should be done with his estate following his death. A will, of course, does not go into effect until after the one who made it (called "the testator") dies. The idea of the death of the maker is seized upon by Bible writers to picture the death of Christ. (See for example Hebrews 9:14-17.)

2. *Decree.* A will or testament contains the will, the desire, of its maker. And sometimes this idea of what the maker wants to happen predominates. A covenant seen in that light is then a decree, the expressed desire of someone capable of enforcing his wish. In Biblical covenants this shows that God gets His will done through the decrees He issues in His covenants.

3. *Contract.* Occasionally we read of a father who willed his son some great fortune on the condition that he take over his father's business, or on the condition that the son must attain a certain age before receiving the sum. This shows that the idea of a covenant sometimes has *conditions attached*; it makes up a contract good only so long as each party keeps his side of the agreement.

Now in speaking of Biblical covenants we are entitled to find traces of each of these meanings of the word *covenant.* Yet we should not push any of them to an extreme. For example, it would be ridiculous to say God has to die before His "testament" can come true!

Jeremiah prophesied the establishment of "a new covenant." The passage runs from Jeremiah 31:31-34, but the heart of it reads: "After those days, saith the Lord, I will put my law in their inward parts, and write it in their hearts; and will be their God, and they shall be my people" (Jeremiah 31:33). In verse 31 this is called "the new covenant."

It is this passage which lies behind the New Testament teaching. For the Gospels (except that of John, who does not report this incident) tell of Jesus identifying the cup with His blood (repeated in 1 Corinthians 11:25); Paul echoes this whole prophecy very clearly in 2 Corinthians 3:1-6; and Hebrews 8:8-12 repeats the entire passage. (Differences in wording are explained, in part, by the fact the Book of Jeremiah was originally written in Hebrew, the Book of Hebrews was written in Greek, and we are reading English translations of both!)

Thus the New Testament finds Jeremiah's prophecy fulfilled in the ministry of Jesus. "Yea, and all the prophets from Samuel and those that follow after, as many as have spoken, have likewise foretold of these days" (Acts 3:24).

INSTITUTED BY JESUS

At the Last Supper Jesus established the "new covenant." "After the same manner also he took the cup, when he had supped, saying, This cup is the new testament in my blood: this do ye, as oft as ye drink it, in remembrance of me" (1 Corinthians 11:25). At this final meal with His disciples the night before He was betrayed, Jesus announced that His blood, to be shed the following day on the cross, signified the arrival of the hope of the prophets—the new covenant.

The "new testament," as the old, involved shedding of blood. "For this is my blood of the new testament, which is shed for many for the remission of sins" (Matthew 26:28; see also Mark 14:24 and Luke 22:20). "Whereupon neither the first testament was dedicated without blood. For when Moses had spoken every precept to all the people according to the law, he took the blood of calves and of goats, with water, and scarlet wool, and hyssop, and sprinkled both the book, and all the people, saying, This is the blood of the testament which God hath enjoined unto you." Thus Hebrews 9:18-20 recounts the covenant-sealing made at Sinai recorded in Exodus 24:3-8. The compelling conclusion is therefore, "If the blood of bulls and of goats, and the ashes of an heifer sprinkling the unclean, sanctifieth to the purifying of the flesh: how much more shall the blood of Christ, who through the eternal Spirit offered himself without spot to God, purge your conscience from dead works to serve the living God?" (Hebrews 9:13,14).

Each meaning of the word *covenant* contributes to an understanding of "the new testament." This new covenant is a *testament,* or will, in that it involved the death (which is what "shedding of blood" stands for) of Christ on the cross. It is a *decree* in that it expresses God's wish that men now be related to Him through this "new and living way" of personal faith in His crucified Son. It is a *contract* in the sense that God promises many blessings to those who will commit themselves to the way of faith and fulfill His specified conditions.

Thus, Jesus brought about a new relationship with God, fulfilling in His death the hope of the prophets. He is, to use a phrase someone has invented, the "Hinge of history."

Contrasted by Paul

It is often possible to discover that doctrines introduced in the Gospels are expanded in the Epistles and consummated in the Revelation. Thus the Revelation speaks of a final, great meal called "the marriage supper of the Lamb" (Revelation 19:9). When He was introducing the rite of the Lord's Supper,

Jesus inserted a forward-looking note: "I will not drink henceforth of this fruit of the vine, until that day when I drink it new with you in my Father's kingdom" (Matthew 26:29). Between the Last Supper and the Marriage Supper, one of which is past and the other yet future, is the Lord's Supper—which looks back to one and forward to the other. And the three meals mark in turn the origination, the continuation, and the consummation of the "new covenant."

When Paul speaks of the new covenant in 1 Corinthians it is in connection with the Corinthian abuse of the Lord's Supper. In 2 Corinthians the situation is different. Here he brings up the new covenant echoing, not Jesus' words as in 1 Corinthians 11:23-26, but Jeremiah's words in the original prophecy. Paul brings up the new covenant here because his opponents apparently were luring the Corinthians back to observance of the Jewish Law (or else to it for the first time in the case of Gentiles). Chapter 3 of 2 Corinthians is therefore Paul's defense: his ministry, a ministry of the new covenant written by the Spirit on hearts instead of cut in stone like the Ten Commandments, is vastly superior to that of Moses'.

In this chapter Paul contrasts the "new testament" with the "old testament" (2 Corinthians 3:14). Although God made (and remade) many covenants with Israel (Romans 9:4), the covenant at Sinai mediated by Moses was the one that gave national unity and purpose to the nation of Israel. Ever after, Moses was recognized as the great lawgiver of Israel. So here Paul picks out this main covenant made with Moses, calls it "the old testament," and then shows the ways in which his own ministry is superior to that of Moses.

1. *A New Material* (2 Corinthians 3:2,3). The old covenant was written first on stone, then with ink on parchment. The new is written by the Spirit on human hearts. Notice here that Paul shows no awareness that there is anything written about the new covenant; its glory lies precisely in the fact that it was unwritten. In the new agreement it is the speaking Spirit, not written laws, which govern man. Yet, in God's oversight, this very letter was eventually to be included in the written and published New Testament.

2. *A New Principle* (2 Corinthians 3:6). The old covenant stressed the letter; the new covenant stressed the Spirit. There is a play on words here, true in Greek as in English. Paul moves from "spirit" in the sense of our expression "the spirit of the law" to the Holy Spirit. Then he expresses a marvelous truth in saying that "the Lord is the Spirit" (2 Corinthians 3:17).

3. *A New Result.* The old led to condemnation and death (2 Corinthians 3:7,9); the new issued in righteousness and life (2 Corinthians 3:6,9).

4. *A New Permanence.* The glory on Moses' face faded (2 Corinthians 3:7); but the Christian gazes at the glory of the Lord disclosed by the Spirit and thus moves from one level of glory to the next (2 Corinthians 3:18).

5. *A New Boldness.* Unlike Moses who used the veil to conceal the fading glow on his face, Paul conceals nothing, uses "great plainness of speech" (2 Corinthians 3:12), and has "renounced the hidden things of dishonesty, not walking in craftiness, nor handling the word of God deceitfully" (2 Corinthians 4:2). His open gospel is "veiled" only to those who reject it (2 Corinthians 4:3,4).

The main point Paul makes here is that his ministry, in contrast to the legalism of his opponents, is supremely one of the Spirit. The Spirit brings life and liberty. And the Spirit is the Lord; that is, Jesus is now present by the Spirit in every believing heart. With steady gaze on Him we are changed by the Spirit to become more and more like Him.

PUBLISHED BY THE CHURCH

But how did this unwritten "new testament" we read about in our printed New Testament ever get into print? The fact that the "old testament" was both written and read (2 Corinthians 3:14) paved the way.

By about A.D. 100 all books of the New Testament were in existence. Near that time, two generations after the Ascension, Revelation was written. But these were all papyrus scrolls, of course, and were written in Greek.

Many other Christian books were also produced by the Christian church. Hints of this appear in Luke 1:1, John 21:5, and Colossians 4:16. When unreliable books began to appear, of which there were many, people began wondering which to believe and which to reject.

Gradually there emerged 27 books in a collection which came to be called "The New Testament." As we have seen, when our printed New Testament speaks of "the new testament" it is not talking about anything in writing. Through the first three and a half centuries the church sifted and sorted the various books. Finally, in the Easter letter of Bishop Athanasius, dated A.D. 367, our 27 books were listed. Accepting these 27 was almost an unconscious, though a God-guided, process. At no time did any official church "council" sit down to decisively define the contents of the New Testament.

Today, we read about God's "new agreement" in neatly printed New Testaments. Printing was not used till the 15th century. The King James Version was printed first in the 17th century, in A.D. 1611. Before printing, people had to consult costly handwritten copies. It should be a matter of constant gratitude on the part of Christians that God has graciously permitted His "new agreement" to become so easily and conveniently available in the printed New Testament.

12

The Cheerful Giver

Read 1 Corinthians 16:1-4; 2 Corinthians 8, 9

The roster of tithers among American industrialists is impressive. Colgate tithed profits on his toothpaste; Heinz, on his soup; Hershey, his chocolate; Kraft, his cheese; Kellogg, his corn flakes; Kerr, his fruit jars; Proctor, his soap; LeTourneau, his earthmovers.

"Thanks be unto God for his unspeakable gift" (2 Corinthians 9:15). With these ringing words of praise Paul closes his two-chapter treatment of Christian giving (2 Corinthians 8 and 9). It is the last word that can be said. For no giving can match God's giving, "for God so loved the world that he gave . . ." (John 3:16). The Corinthians, of all people, knew about spiritual gifts (1 Corinthians 12:1); they "came behind in no gift" (1 Corinthians 1:7). They were a gifted people serving a giving God. But they lacked one thing.

In 2 Corinthians 8 and 9 we see the same stubborn spirit so evident throughout 1 Corinthians. In the first letter (1 Corinthians 16:1-4) Paul invited the Corinthians to participate in a fundraising project for poor Jewish Christians in Jerusalem. They agreed. But now a year or so had passed (2 Corinthians 9:2). We get the idea that their good intentions had become throttled, very likely due to the upset in the church caused by the intruding "super-apostles" who belittled Paul.

Unfulfilled intentions have a curiously modern application too. And from Paul's words to the reneging Corinthians we can readily extract a whole philosophy of Christian giving.

One thing about this project of Paul: it was a sort of foreign missions in reverse. He was collecting from the churches established on the field in order to assist the home church in Jerusalem that had mothered them in the beginning. But he reasoned this way: "For if the Gentiles have been made partakers of their spiritual things, their duty is also to minister unto them in carnal things" (Romans 15:27).

PRECEDENTS TO GIVING

Just what is the background to this collection for the poor that Paul refers to?

1. *The saints in the Jerusalem church were poor.* The church started in Jerusalem where, on the first Christian Pentecost, its membership suddenly zoomed to more than 3,000 (Acts 2:41). For a Jew to become a Christian meant, then as now, probable disownment by family and friends. His business would fall off rapidly. His means of support by himself or by his family was then threatened.

At first the church met this need by living in common: possessions were sold and the proceeds equitably distributed (Acts 2:44,45). When Barnabas joined the Christian movement he sold his property and turned the money over to the apostles (Acts 4:36,37). In sharp contrast Ananias and Sapphira fatally attempted to cheat the Holy Spirit (Acts 5:1-11).

About a dozen years after the Ascension, Agabus predicted that a great famine would soon occur, as it did under the reign of Emperor Claudius Caesar, who ruled A.D. 41 to 54. This of course further impoverished the Jerusalem saints. "Then the disciples, every man according to his ability, determined to send relief unto the brethren which dwelt in Judea" (Acts 11:29). As the following verse (Acts 11:30) indicates, Paul took this collection to Jerusalem along with Barnabas.

2. *Throughout his ministry Paul was always concerned with the famine fund.* The famine-fund visit to Jerusalem described in Acts 11:29,30 took place about A.D. 46. This was before any of his famed missionary journeys. After all these journeys were completed, in his defense before Felix around A.D. 59, we hear Paul saying, "Now after many years I came to bring alms to my nation, and offerings" (Acts 24:17).

Within these "many years" Paul presented this matter to the Galatian churches (1 Corinthians 16:1, probably referring to the churches he founded at Antioch in Pisidia, Lystra, Derbe, and the surrounding area as described in Acts 13 and 14). He had also stressed the project among the "Macedonian" churches (Romans 15:26; 2 Corinthians 8:1-5). Macedonia was the area to the north of Achaia in Greece which included the cities and therefore the churches at Philippi, Berea, and Thessalonica—churches founded on his second mission.

Now we find him urging the matter upon the Corinthians. The whole story has a happy ending. For when Paul wrote the Book of Romans—which he did while at Corinth when he fulfilled his promise in 2 Corinthians to come to them (the Corinthians)—he wrote to the brethren at Rome that he expected to come to Rome after he stopped at Jerusalem. And the reason he gives for going to Jerusalem is this: "For it hath pleased them of Macedonia and Achaia to make a certain contribution for the poor saints which are at Jerusalem" (Romans 15:26).

The project of raising funds for the poor at Jerusalem was therefore a major effort of the beginning church. Every Jew scattered throughout the Mediterranean world was regularly taxed for the support of the Jerusalem temple. So there was a kind of precedent for the project. It was a beautiful way of manifesting the unity of the church Paul wrote about to the Corinthians who were divided among themselves. The Gentile Christians, ministered to by the gospel that came through the Jews, now minister to the material needs of the Christian Jews.

3. *The famine fund was a special mission project and did not relate to the support of the local church.* There is little said in the New Testament about just how the local churches were supported. For example we read about this famine fund, but we are told nothing about their tithing practices.

Paul put great stress on the obligation of the church to support its ministry—even though he himself renounced that right at Corinth (1 Corinthians 9:1-15). Some mechanism for the efficient collection and distribution of funds for the local needs of the church must have existed.

The important thing to see is that here in the famine fund details are helpful hints for Christian giving. And Christian giving begins with gratitude for God's gifts. It is a matter of a willing heart, not of a bound conscience. If any man wants to argue that tithing is, or is not, binding upon the Christian, he may do so. There are some who feel it does not apply. Notice that Paul moves along an entirely different plane in expounding his philosophy of giving.

Second Corinthians 8 and 9 let us catch Paul's philosophy of giving. Stated in language aimed at ourselves, a list of suggested hints emerging from this passage would look like this:

1. *Start with giving yourself.* The Macedonians, Paul explains by holding them up as an example to the Corinthians, "first gave their own selves to the Lord, and unto us by the will of God" (2 Corinthians 8:5). Before they undertook to be giving their moneys to others, they put first things first; they made a total commitment to God first. The Lord is never interested in our money because He or His Church is broke! He owns everything anyway: "For the earth is the Lord's and the fulness thereof" (1 Corinthians 10:26, quoting Psalm 24:1).

If we fail to give, His Church will not crumble. Rather, he offers us an opportunity to share in the work He is doing in the world. When people give themselves to God, they become anxious to help others at their own expense. So if we give ourselves to God we will then readily give our goods to His Church—just like the Macedonians.

2. *Give in the midst of poverty or troubles.* Of these exemplary Macedonians Paul remarked "How that in a great trial of affliction the abundance of their joy and their deep poverty abounded unto the riches of their liberality" (2 Corinthians 8:2). They had their own difficulties, perhaps including financial reverses, but they still found it possible to give. Once again we see that the important thing is not how much we give, but how we give—not the

111

amount, but the attitude. To hear Jesus speak, one would think that giving is receiving: "Give, and it shall be given unto you" (Luke 6:38). "It is more blessed to give than to receive" (Acts 20:35).

3. *Give regularly and gradually.* Sometimes it is tempting to postpone giving till some indefinite great moment of giving that is way off in the future. Paul advised the Corinthians—and apparently the Galatians as well—"Upon the first day of the week let every one of you lay by him in store . . ." (1 Corinthians 16:2). It is better for our giving to be small and regular than to be large and irregular, as the old fable of the tortoise and the hare confirms.

4. *Decide the amount of your gift personally and sensibly.* The frequency of this guideline to giving is amazing. The early disciples gave to the first famine fund "every man according to his ability" (Acts 11:29; perhaps the key lies in the phrase "every man!"). When Paul first brought up the subject to the Corinthians he said they each should set something aside "as God hath prospered him" (1 Corinthians 16:2). In the second letter (2 Corinthians 8:8), when he brings up the matter again he says he is not speaking "by commandment," he is not demanding this of them but inviting them to participate. The full statement of this principle comes in 2 Corinthians 9:7 in words which are crystal-clear: "Every man according as he purposeth in his heart, so let him give; not grudgingly, or of necessity: for God loveth a cheerful giver."

So the amount we give is a matter of personal decision. It should be based on ability and resolve. We could expect that the amount would increase with the personal spiritual development of each believer; there are certainly many testimonies of financial improvement following faith-prompted giving. But again, the willing heart is central. "For if there be first a willing mind, it is accepted according to that a man hath, and not according to that he hath not" (2 Corinthians 8:12).

For many people, Christian giving is a matter of tithing—which means giving a tenth of one's income. Abundant testimonies confirm the blessing of determining to return this proportion of one's income to the Lord. But tithing should never become a matter of bondage. Even tithing means nothing unless it is done in the right spirit.

5. *Keep to your pledge!* A year earlier the Corinthians had promised to help, but they were tardy. So Paul writes: "And now complete the doing also, in order that, just as there was then the eagerness in desiring, there may now be the accomplishment in proportion to your means" (2 Corinthians 8:11, Weymouth). If some things are easier said than done, pledges are easier made than paid! "Now therefore perform the doing of it!"

6. *Make room for fundraisers!* Let no one think fundraising is out of place in the church! Titus had this job at Corinth (2 Corinthians 8:6). Paul refers to two other unnamed brothers he is sending with Titus to complete arrangements for the collection in Corinth and then he gives specific instructions on how to treat fundraisers: "Wherefore shew ye to them, and before the churches, the proof of your love, and of our boasting on your behalf" (2 Corinthians 8:24).

PRINCIPLES FOR GIVING

The procedures for the practical side of giving rest on certain principles. Paul mentions these. They are true facts which lie behind Christian giving and provide it with meaning and purpose. Here are these principles.

1. *Sharing makes things even.* "For it is not [intended] that other people be used and relieved (of their responsibility) and you be burdened and suffer (unfairly), but to have equality—share and share alike; your surplus over necessity at the present time going to meet their want and to equalize the difference created by it, so that [at some other time] their surplus in turn may be given to supply your want. Thus there may be equality" (2 Corinthians 8:13,14, *Amplified New Testament*). Giving is not intended to put givers under undue stress; the opposite is true. It evens things up.

2. *Sparse sowing means sparse reaping.* Sowing much seed means harvesting much grain. Much giving, much receiving. "Give, and it shall be given unto you; good measure, pressed down, and shaken together, and running over, shall men give into your bosom. For with the same measure that ye mete withal it shall be measured to you again" (Luke 6:38).

3. *Willingness excels quantity.* "It's not what you give," the saying goes, "but what you have left." The willing giver "whose heart stirs him up" is the blessed giver, regardless of the size of his gift.

4. *God blesses givers.* This is a simple truth which, for that very reason, might be overlooked. Paul states it this way: "After all, God can give you everything that you need, so that you may always have sufficient both for yourselves and for giving away to other people. The more you are enriched by God, the more scope will there be for generous giving" (2 Corinthians 9:8,11, Phillips).

5. *Giving to others is giving to God.* "For the ad-

114

ministration of this service not only supplieth the want of the saints, but is abundant also by many thanksgivings unto God" (2 Corinthians 9:12). "And the King shall answer and say unto them, Verily I say unto you, Inasmuch as ye have it unto one of the least of these my brethren, ye have done it unto me" (Matthew 25:40; compare verse 45).

It is this kind of unselfish, blessed giving to which Paul invited the Corinthians. If they would willingly, of their own accord, follow his hints they would see these principles come true.

PERSPECTIVES ON GIVING

In Paul's approach to the Corinthians to get them to fulfill their earlier promises, he appealed to them from various standpoints. He sought to awaken motives within them that would stimulate their participation in the famine fund. These motives he views from the following perspectives, each with a lesson for giving today.

1. *Self.* "Therefore, as ye abound in every thing, in faith, and utterance, and knowledge, and in all diligence, and in your love to us, see that ye abound in this grace also" (2 Corinthians 8:7, compare 1 Corinthians 1:7). How tactfully the apostle speaks! He appeals to their integrity, asking them to be consistent here as they are elsewhere—certainly a compliment in the light of 1 Corinthians.

2. *Others.* The example of others has significance. An interesting fact emerges. Paul was setting the example of the Macedonians before the Corinthians (2 Corinthians 8:1-5) and he was setting the example of the Corinthians before the Macedonians (2 Corinthians 9:1-5)! So he used each to stimulate the other! There were many things he could have told

115

the Macedonians about the Corinthians. But instead, he commended their example.

3. *Christ.* "For ye know the grace of our Lord Jesus Christ, that, though he was rich, yet for your sakes he became poor, that ye through his poverty might be rich" (2 Corinthians 8:9, which is Philippians 2:5-11 in miniature). When it comes to giving, what example can match the Lord Jesus?

4. *God.* "Thanks be unto God for his unspeakable gift" (2 Corinthians 9:15). Every good gift comes from the Father above (James 1:17). But no gift of His approaches the gift of His Son. God gave His only begotten Son. The Son gave himself. Into this fellowship of giving, the believer enters by first giving himself.

13

The Apostle Extraordinary

Read 2 Corinthians 10-13

The Man Paul

Paul, a modern writer somewhere observed, would have been a great personality in history even had he never met Christ. His personality was that forceful, his gifts that ample. But any Christian knows that an unchristian Paul is an unthinkable thought. God had long ago planned the arrival in the young church of this devoted man of God. Outside of Christ himself, no figure looms so large in the pages of the New Testament as that of Paul.

Who is this remarkable man? What did he look like? What were the secrets of his personality and dedication? How did he react to the stern and persistent opposition he met on every hand? What did his pursuit of Christ cost him personally? Deeper answers to these questions come only by thoroughly reading and rereading the letters he left, which make up half the total number of books in the New Testament.

But a start can be made, for the Corinthian letters we have scanned in this book are precisely those letters that show us the apostle inside and out, his inner thoughts and his outer labors. As a final stage in this series on the Corinthian correspondence, we look at the pastor of the Church of God, the assembly of God, in that ancient, wicked city—Corinth.

117

What did the apostle Paul look like? This is a question of interest, but one nowhere directly answered in the Bible. We are not told of the appearance of Jesus, despite modern paintings of Him. We only know of the Lord that at the beginning of His ministry He must have looked "about thirty years of age" (Luke 3:23), though the Jews at one time took Him as "not yet fifty years old" (John 8:57). So also we can get from the Bible only a general picture of Paul.

Apparently, Paul did not present a particularly handsome appearance. A significant verse repeats the charges of his critics. "For his letters, say they, are weighty and powerful; but his bodily presence is weak, and his speech contemptible" (2 Corinthians 10:10). Paul responds with the assurance that he will be in presence what his letters are in his absence. But he makes no point of boasting of his physical appearance. Instead, he glories in weakness. He admits that he was weak in speaking (1 Corinthians 2:1,3; 2 Corinthians 11:6). Though the nature of the thorn given him is nowhere detailed (2 Corinthians 12:7), it may have been a physical blemish according to some scholarly guesses. The overall impression of Paul's physical appearance is then that of one whose chief attraction lies in the force of his personality, however he may have appeared. He was, we might say, more spirit than body.

Early church history supplies a description of Paul. About a hundred years or so after the death of the apostle there appeared a document attempting to recount the *Acts of Paul* and bearing that title. The reliability of this writing is not high, but it contains the only account of the physical appearance of Paul that has come down to us. The account, supposed to have originated with Titus, reads in this manner:

"And he saw Paul coming, a man of little stature, thin-haired upon the head, crooked in the legs, of good state of body, with eyebrows joining, and nose somewhat hooked, full of grace: for sometimes he appeared like a man, and sometimes he had the face of an angel."

Such an account of course cannot be depended upon as would a Biblical account. But it is interesting to note that the name Paul, taken by the apostle sometime after his conversion, comes from a Latin word meaning "small." Whether or not this reflected the small stature of the apostle we of course cannot know. Fortunately, we do not need to know.

PAUL'S CHARACTERISTICS

It is far easier, and much more profitable, to consider the traits of the converted rabbi. It would prove to be an interesting task—and a quite possible one —to trace in the Corinthian letters evidences in their author of each of the fruit of the Spirit listed in Galatians 5:22,23. But here we may itemize several significant characteristics of this remarkable man. He was a man of:

1. *Deep Spiritual Experience.* Long before he met Christ, Paul was a religious man and a trained professional Jewish rabbi. Then came that life-changing appearance of Christ to him on the Damascus Road (1 Corinthians 15:8; Acts 9:1-22). With the same vigor with which he persecuted he now preached. Life to him became but one thing, or rather, one Person. "For to me to live is Christ" (Philippians 1:21). After Paul's conversion, he was filled with the Holy Spirit (Acts 9:17). It is remarkable to find

him telling the Corinthians, in the light of their excessive abuse of the gifts of the Spirit, that he spoke with tongues more than all of them (1 Corinthians 14:18).

Though forced to boast of his apostolic qualifications, Paul says he would merely mention deep spiritual experiences involving revelations and hearing "unspeakable words, which it is not lawful for a man to utter" (2 Corinthians 12:1-6). There is an intimacy, a privacy, about deeper spiritual experience which is not always observed by followers of the apostle. Paul was a man of unusual spiritual depth and perception.

2. *Total Dedication.* Paul was not one who became active only after his conversion. As a zealous Jewish rabbi he hotly opposed the new movement rising within Palestine. Others could go about their business, but he must secure letters from the Sanhedrin and seize these Christians, "entering into every house, and haling men and women," then carrying them off to prison (Acts 8:3).

We are not told what was the effect on Paul of the radiant faces of his prisoners, their unaccounted willingness to die for the heretical Jewish Carpenter. But we do know that the same zeal was channeled into the service of Christ. It would take him to any extreme. "If meat make my brother to offend, I will eat no flesh while the world standeth, lest I make my brother to offend" (1 Corinthians 8:13); "for though I be free from all men, yet have I made myself servant unto all, that I might gain the more" (1 Corinthians 9:19).

Even life itself no longer matters: "We are confident, I say, and willing rather to be absent from the body, and to be present with the Lord" (2 Corinthians 5:8). What he wrote the Roman church as he sat in Corinth is typical: "As much as in me is, I am ready to preach the gospel to you that are at Rome also" (Romans 1:15).

3. *Knowledge and Tact.* Moses, Daniel, Paul— these were three men of God who were university men, well trained in the schools of their day. They were men whom God used in powerfully significant ways in His dealings with His people. Paul the rabbi had been trained, not only in the contents of the Scriptures which show on every page of his letters, but in the methods of thought and argument as well. Yet all this he was prepared to set aside for the higher knowledge, the personal knowledge of Jesus Christ. But no reader of Paul's letters will fail to discern how God used the learning of the rabbi in the writing of the apostle. And tact? "Brethren," he addresses them, when he is about to reprove their divisive factions (1 Corinthians 1:10). And Timothy, he says, will gently "remind" them of his ways in Christ (1 Corinthians 4:17).

4. *Loving Pastoral Patience.* At the cost of being charged with fickleness (2 Corinthians 1:15-17), Paul changed his intention of coming to the Corinthians in order to spare them a humbling and embarrassing situation (2 Corinthians 1:23). Though he wrote Second Corinthians to prepare for his third trip to them, he still feared that his arrival would bring severe action toward the persistent offenders (2 Corinthians 12:20,21). We see in the great apostle, not only the author of the great chapter on love but also the conscientious pastor who, when the extent of unrepentance warrants, can advise turning an offending brother over to Satan (1 Corinthians 5:5). There is

a time when the health of the body demands amputation of a part of it.

5. *Forthright Honesty.* Because he accepted no support from the Corinthians, some of his critics accused Paul of "taking a cut" from the collection after it was secured by Titus (2 Corinthians 12:17, 18). But Paul's practice in handling of funds called for "providing for honest things, not only in the sight of the Lord, but also in the sight of men" (2 Corinthians 8:21). Furthermore, he was honest in handling the Word of God (2 Corinthians 4:1,2)—a point for preachers to ponder who "use texts for pretexts"!

PAUL'S ENEMIES

One of the costs of leadership is opposition. This is no less true in Christian leadership, Paul had enemies—

1. *In the Church.* "I'll take care of my enemies," the saying goes, "God save me from my friends." Those in the Corinthian church who said they were "of Paul" had pushed the apostle's preaching of freedom from the Law over to an unwarranted libertine extreme.

2. *In the Ministry.* Because reading 2 Corinthians is like hearing one side of a telephone conversation, it is difficult to understand some of the things said there. But we clearly discern competitive preachers at Corinth. A verse from the *Amplified New Testament* makes this clear: "For [you seem readily to endure it] if a man comes and preaches another Jesus than the One we preached, or if you receive a different spirit from the [Spirit] you [once] received, or a different gospel from the one you [then] received and welcomed. You tolerate [all that] well enough! Yet I consider myself as in no way inferior

to these (precious) extra-super [false] apostles" (2 Corinthians 11:4,5).

3. *In the World.* The opposition of the Jews against their former rabbi is recorded in 2 Corinthians 11:24 and Acts 14:19. Look at his difficulties described in Acts 14:5,6; 16:19-25.

4. *In the Universe.* According to Philippians 2:10,11 and Colossians 1:11; 2:15, Paul believed that spirit powers lurked invisibly behind the ordered universe. We see this belief also in his discussion about "the table of devils" (1 Corinthians 10:20) and possibly when he speaks about the Crucifixion (1 Corinthians 2:8, where *princes* may refer to evil spirits).

PAUL'S PRINCIPLES

What were the secrets of this unusual man? We can hardly do better in discovering them than to look at some of his key thoughts expressed in his own words as taken from the Corinthian letters:

1. *"Jesus Christ, and him crucified"* (1 Corinthians 2:2). At the center of Paul's Christian experience, as at the forefront of his preaching, reigned the crucified Lord of Glory. This was foolishness in the eyes of human wisdom, but after all, that is all one could expect. For the Cross was God's secret design.

2. *"When I am weak, then am I strong"* (2 Corinthians 12:10). What work he did, so he explained (1 Corinthians 15:10), was not done by him at all, but by the inward grace of God. He could not boast of strength before the accusers at Corinth; but he learned that real strength comes only through weakness. Only when man is weak can God be strong in him.

3. *"He that glorieth, let him glory in the Lord"* (1 Corinthians 1:31; 2 Corinthians 10:17). Human wisdom and argument are wrong because they are but another variety of human boasting. Whoever must boast (and that will be rare) must boast in the Lord.

4. *"I seek not yours, but you"* (2 Corinthians 12:14). Here is Paul's secret for pastors. He did not seek their money, their praise, their loyalty. He sought them—men for whom Christ died, men with whom he pleaded that they be reconciled to God. He was not in business for himself. He was Christ's ambassador.

5. *"We are perplexed, but not in despair"* (2 Corinthians 4:8). The joys of the Christian run deep. They are unspeakable. On the surface are often disappointment and baffling circumstances. But these never reach the deep running waters of peace.

6. *"We must all appear before the judgment seat of Christ"* (2 Corinthians 5:10). This theme recurs a surprising number of times in the Corinthian letters, and therefore must have been one of the compelling motives of the apostle. The idea controls the thoughts expressed in 1 Corinthians 3:13; 2 Corinthians 1:14; 5:11. When first in Corinth, Paul had been hailed before the judgment seat of the governor, Gallio (Acts 18:12). So both he and the Corinthians knew what appearing before a judgment seat was like!

7. *"Do all to the glory of God"* (1 Corinthians 10:31). The arrival of faith in the heart brings vast relief and freedom. No entangling legalism can ever again entrap one freed by Jesus. But in expressing this liberty, the believer must observe the twin rules —God's glory and men's profit. By the profit of men

Paul means "that they may be saved" (1 Corinthians 10:33).

PAUL'S SELF-ESTIMATE

Paul held a very honest opinion of himself. He neither boasted that he was more than he was. Nor did he belittle what God had done through him. Though he recognized, frankly, that he worked harder than any of the apostles, he knew this was not his own doing but the result of God's grace through him (1 Corinthians 15:10).

He regarded himself the product of God's grace. "By the grace of God I am what I am" (1 Corinthians 15:10). This was his life motto. See how he opened his letter to the Corinthians: "Paul, an apostle of Jesus Christ by the will of God." It was God's plan, God's guidance, God's power that worked through him.

He made no apologies for himself. He knew that what he was—his inabilities and weaknesses as well as his accomplishments—all came from God's grace in his life. No pot ever asks its maker why he made it that way. It merely does its job without asking questions (Romans 9:20). This treasure Paul had in an earthen vessel. But he was far more concerned with God's treasure than with his vessel. Yet God had whispered to Ananias about Paul: "He is a chosen vessel unto me" (Acts 9:15).